This book belongs to

Olivia

a young woman of prayer.

From Nana 2013

A Young Woman's Guide to Prayer

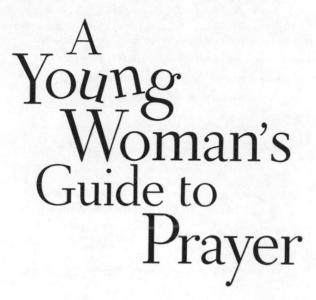

ELIZABETH GEORGE

HARVEST HOUSE PUBLISHERS
EUGENE, OREGON

Cover by Dugan Design Group, Bloomington, Minnesota

Cover photos © iStockphoto/murnamoo; cedrov/Fotolia

Acknowledgment

As always, thank you to my dear husband, Jim George, M.Div., Th.M., for your able assistance, guidance, suggestions, and loving encouragement on this project.

A YOUNG WOMAN'S GUIDE TO PRAYER
Copyright © 2005, 2012 by Elizabeth George
Published by Harvest House Publishers
Eugene, Oregon 97402
www.harvesthousepublishers.com

ISBN 978-0-7369-4499-1 (pbk.)
ISBN 978-0-7369-4500-4 (eBook)

Printed in the United States of America

12 13 14 15 16 17 18 / BP-KB / 9 8 7 6 5 4 3 2 1

Contents

Developing the Habit of Prayer

Answering God's Call to Prayer

Become a Young Woman of Prayer

Talking to God about the issues of your life is important...and prayer is the key! But if you're like most women—old or young!—you can use a little help with your prayer-life. That's why I've written this practical book—to help you make your desire to pray regularly a reality.

The journey to a dynamic and authentic prayer-life is an exciting adventure! First, you'll find out what God says about prayer in the Bible. It's awesome! You'll also enjoy stories from the hearts and lives of Bible characters. These people learned to pray...loved to pray...and witnessed the mighty effects of prayer and its impact on their relationship with God. Along with insights from my own prayer journey, I share inspiring examples of others who have answered God's call to prayer. You'll discover tips for revolutionizing your own personal prayer-life, including...

> ...*12 practical ways to become a woman of prayer*—You'll discover what to do...and what not to do. And you'll understand why prayer can be so difficult to do!

    ... *"My Checklists for Prayer"*—Each chapter gives three immediate prayer-steps you can take—today!—to make your dream of becoming a woman of prayer come true.

    ... *"Would You Like to Know More?"*—If you want to "put the icing on the cake" of prayer, you can grow even more by interacting with a few additional scriptures and questions. They are tailor-made just for you!

    ... *"Things I Don't Want to Forget"*—Every chapter has exciting life-changing suggestions for your everyday life...if you don't forget them! So to help you remember what speaks most to your heart, I've added a special page at the end of each chapter for you to journal or record your thoughts and "take-away truths." Your written personal insights will become a testimony of your spiritual growth, a cherished keepsake you can refer to in the days, months, and even years ahead.

    ... *"My Prayer Calendar"*—I've also put a reproducible prayer calendar at the back of this book. It will help you see how you're becoming a woman of prayer. Be sure you make a photocopy because you'll want to use it year after year...and share it with your friends!

Dear praying friend, as you grow in prayer, and as prayer becomes more and more a part of your life, you'll find God becoming your closest friend. And you'll find He can help you with *everything* that's important in your life right now and always—your family, your friends, your school, and your dreams for the future.

So journey on! Read and study this book alone, or go through it with a friend, a mentor, or in a group. Whichever way you choose, you'll be blessed. Why? Because prayer is the "highest activity of which the human spirit is capable."[1] Through prayer you...

—worship God...and express your love for Him,

—bring your needs before God...and see how He answers, and

—talk one-on-one with the God of the universe...about your life.

My precious new friend, I am praying for you right now as you answer God's call...to pray!

In His great and amazing love,
Your friend and sister in Christ,

Elizabeth George

Making
Your
Desire to Pray
a Reality

Beginning Your Journey into Prayer

Prayer.

Just say the word and I begin to yearn and squirm at the same time. As a woman after God's own heart, I *yearn* to pray. My soul longs for it. My spirit craves communion with my heavenly Father. My heart sings with the words of King David found in the Old Testament:

> As the deer pants for streams of water, so my soul pants for you, O God....My soul thirsts for you; my body longs for you" (Psalm 42:1; 63:1).

And yet I also *squirm* at the thought of prayer. Why? Because even though prayer is a blessing, approaching our holy, holy, holy God is also an awesome thing. Then there is the search for time to get alone with God to talk with Him.

> "We're not talking to a brick wall when we pray—we're talking to Someone who really listens."[1]

What a battle! I know that I need to pray...and I want to pray! And yet the work and the discipline praying calls for is quite real! Do you, my dear new friend, share these same mixed feelings? Then let's decide to answer God's call to us to be women of prayer...no matter what! Let's embark on a journey together to learn more about prayer. Let's seek to live our lives "on bended knee."

Hearing God's Call to Prayer

On any journey, a first step must always be taken. What will your first step be? I remember my first step into seriously learning how to pray. It was on Mother's Day, May 8, 1983. My daughter Katherine (age 13) gave me the gift of a tiny wordless book. It was purple...and I still have it because it's a real keepsake to me. It's special, first of all, because my daughter gave it to me! (That really touches a mother's heart! Trust me on this one.)

Anyway, Katherine had the idea for the gift and arranged with Jim (my husband and Kath's dad) to do extra work chores to earn the money to purchase it for me. Then the two of them went off together to shop for just the right present for Mom. The little treasure was then inscribed by Katherine on the bookplate in her careful handwriting, lovingly gift wrapped, and proudly given to me on that Sunday morning so many years ago.

Oh, believe me, I screamed! I squealed! I did everything but turn cartwheels to express my thanks to my sweet daughter. But then I faced a problem—what to do with a wordless book. For several months I let the small book lie on the coffee table so my dear Katherine would know how much I truly appreciated it. Then one day, not knowing exactly what to do with it, I moved it into the book-case...and it was gone forever....

...until September 12, four months later. That day was my tenth birthday in the Lord. As I sat alone before God, I looked back over my first ten years as God's child. Of course, that led to a time of thanking Him for His mercy, His grace, His care, His guidance, His wisdom, my salvation through Christ....

On and on my prayers of appreciation to God gushed. Then after dabbing my eyes with a tissue, I turned my thoughts forward and I prayed, "Lord, as I start a new decade with You, is there anything missing from my Christian life that I should focus on for the next ten years?"

Oh, dear friend, I can only report to you that before I put the question mark on the question, I knew in my heart what the answer was! It was *prayer*! And suddenly I knew I had "heard" God's call to prayer in my heart. And just as suddenly, I knew what to do with that tiny purple wordless book. I ran to the bookcase, pulled it out, opened it up, and wrote on the very first page:

> I dedicate and purpose to spend the next ten
> years in the Lord, Lord willing, developing a
> meaningful prayer life.

Making a Commitment

Why did I pick ten years for my commitment to develop a meaningful prayer life? Probably because it was my tenth birthday in Christ. And those ten years have come and gone. And I want to tell to you right now—I am *still* learning how to pray! You know, you and I don't just wake up one day at the point where we can mark "learn to pray" off our to-do list!

"Lord, teach us to pray" (Luke 11:1).

No, no one prays enough. And no one prays as passionately as she would like to pray or should pray. And no one prays for as many people as need to be prayed for.

And so we must continue on our journey into prayer until we "get it," until we can even say that we've *begun* to know even a little bit about prayer. And until that happens, a lot of Christians pray what I call "Christopher Robin" prayers. He's the little boy who struggled with his evening "Vespers."[2] Little Christopher became so distracted by anything and everything that he couldn't remember who or what to pray for. So he ended up praying "God bless _____" prayers, filling in the blank with the names of his family and friends.

Boy oh boy, can I ever relate to Christopher Robin's "prayer" experience! And maybe you can, too! That's exactly how I prayed...that is, before my commitment to answer God's call to pray. Yes, that's how I had prayed. And, like Christopher Robin, my mind wandered. I didn't know who to pray for...or how to pray for them. So my prayers basically consisted of lame efforts, until they finally wound down to a muttered "God bless me and my family today."

But, praise God, I can say that some progress has been made! I believe that my prayers and my prayer-life have improved. But I want to quickly say, "No, I have not yet arrived." Being a woman of prayer is still a daily challenge and constant struggle for me. And I imagine it will be that way until I see my Savior face-to-face.

In the chapters to come, we'll go deeper into what it means to answer God's call to prayer. But for now (and at the end of each chapter), I want you to pause and consider some practical steps you can take *right now*. They will help you to grow a heart for prayer and grow in your heart-relationship with God. I left some space for you to write your answers.

My Checklist for Prayer

✓ *Pray now!*—It's one thing to read about prayer. And oh, how we love to talk about prayer! And oh, how we dream about being women of prayer! But it's quite another thing to actually pray. So *Step 1* is this: Put your book down, grab a kitchen timer, and go somewhere where you can shut the door or be alone. Then pray for five minutes. Use these five golden minutes to pour out your heart's desire to your heavenly Father. Tell Him how much you love Him. And tell Him how much you long to answer His call upon your life to become—and be!—a woman of prayer. Then share here a little about what happened.

✓   *Get organized*—Round up some kind of notebook. It can be anything—a spiral pad, a three-ring binder, even a little wordless book. Whatever it is, do what you can to make your notebook personal and fun. Make it something you want to use. For instance, is your favorite color purple? Then make your prayer notebook a purple one! (And don't forget to include a pen with purple ink!) And don't worry about your choice being permanent. Also don't get hung up on needing to make the "right" choice. Just choose something—anything!—that will help you and inspire you to take your first steps down the path of your journey into prayer.

I just looked in my own little purple wordless book, and based on dates, I used it for ten weeks. Ten weeks is a l-o-n-g time, which means that little book was enough to launch my commitment to learn to pray. That also means using my book for ten weeks was long enough to show me I needed a different kind of notebook.

This will probably happen to you too, as you begin your prayer efforts. But be excited when it does! Praise God you are growing in your prayer skills…and look forward to creating a fresh, new, made-by-you prayer notebook.

Describe your current notebook or journal. What do you like about it? Do you need to make any improvements?

✓ *Look ahead*—Look over…and pray over…the next week on your calendar. What is the pattern of your life, your daily routine? What are your school and work commitments? What kind of time do you need for family and friends? Then mark on each day for the next week the exact time you will schedule as your prayer time. It can be the same time each day, or it can be customized to fit the demands and flow of each individual day.

Next mark your prayer appointments in ink on your calendar. Then, of course, be sure you keep them…just like you keep your dates with your friends! As one of my prayer principles says, "There is no right or wrong way to pray…except not to pray!"

For a place to record your prayer progress, I've provided a "My Prayer Calendar" in the back of this book. Just shade in the squares for the days you do pray, and leave those blank when you don't pray. And then, my dear praying friend, one picture is worth a thousand words! All you have to do is glance at the "My Prayer Calendar"…and the tale of your times in prayer will be told! Now, what tale will your efforts in prayer tell?

What do you dream will be true of your "Prayer Calendar"? And what can you do today to make your dream a reality?

✎ Answering God's Call to You

Prayer is truly the queen of all the habits we could desire as women of faith. As we leave this chapter about "Beginning Steps in Prayer," I want you to take this thought with you.

> He who has learned how to pray
> has learned the greatest secret
> of a holy and a happy life.[3]

I'm sure you caught the word "learned." But I hope and pray you also caught the reward, too. All of your learning and efforts in prayer will help lead you to "a holy and a happy life"! And the beautiful miracle is that a holy and a happy life can be yours each day...one day at a time...as you answer God's call to pray. So let the outpourings of your heart begin now—*today*! The opportunity and privilege of talking to God through prayer is yours...*if* that is the desire of your heart and *if* you act on that desire.

Now, what will your beginning steps be?

Would You Like to Know More? Check It Out!

We'll look at these topics later in our book, but for now, what do these verses from the Bible tell you about prayer and your prayer-life?

Matthew 6:6—

Matthew 7:7-8—

Luke 18:1—

Romans 12:12—

Ephesians 6:18—

Philippians 4:6-7—

Colossians 4:2—

1 Thessalonians 5:17—

1 Peter 3:12—

My Commitment to Prayer

What commitment to prayer will you make? Write it here. (And remember, it doesn't have to be long. Just a few sincere words can change a life...and a heart!)

_____

_____

_____

_____

_____

_____

_____

_____

_____

_____

_____

_____

_____

                                                    (Signed)

                                                    (Date)

My List of Things I Don't Want to Forget...
...from This Chapter

2

What Keeps Me
from Praying?

Why is it that so many of the things we as responsible women—young or old—must tend to in life are hard to do? And if they're not hard to do, they are at least hard to get started on? Take, for instance, getting out of bed in the morning. For me, this is one of those hard-to-do things (and I'm sure you agree!). Then begins a day-long list of people to see and places to go.

On and on the list of a busy gal's "musts" and "have-to's" goes—a list of important things that are necessary and that others depend on us to do.

But "The Most Vital and Important Thing" that we as God's women "must" get around to and "have to" include in our every day is *prayer*. No matter how difficult our personal and school work is, it is even harder to do the *spiritual* work of prayer! If we aren't careful, we can spend all day—and all night—doing less-important tasks—anything!— to put off the most-difficult-yet-most-rewarding "task" of all—praying.

There's not a doubt in our minds that prayer is critical to every part of our lives. So why is it so hard for us to pray?

After thinking through the Scriptures and looking at my own heart and life, I've discovered some reasons—and excuses—for not praying.

1. *Worldliness*—We live "in the world" (John 17:11), and the world affects us more than we think. It daily bombards us with "everything in the world— the cravings of sinful man, the lust of his eyes and the boasting of what he has and does," all of which "comes not from the Father but from the world" (1 John 2:16). Not one voice in the world is telling us to take care of spiritual things. And prayer is a *spiritual* exercise.

   So watch out for the world! Resist the world by watching in prayer (Matthew 26:41). As the hymn writer expressed it, "Turn your eyes upon Jesus… and the things of earth will grow strangely dim in the light of His glory and grace."[1]

2. *Busyness*—Another reason we don't pray is because we just don't take the time to pray. And usually the culprit is busyness. Don't get me wrong! The Bible says a strong work ethic is a mark of strong character.

   But the Bible also shows us in the story of two sisters named Martha and Mary that a priority order must be set between our *spiritual* duties and our *daily* duties. (You can read about them in Luke 10:38-42.) In a nutshell, Martha was a very busy woman who did a lot of good things…but carried them to such an extreme that she "lost it" on the glorious day when Jesus came to visit. She literally fell apart when her sister stopped her kitchen work to go sit at the feet of Jesus, God-in-flesh!

Both sisters loved Jesus, and both gladly served Him. But Mary knew when to stop with the busyness and do the best thing, the *one thing* that's most important—spend time with God. And, dear sister, you and I must do the same.

> "A woman who is too busy to pray is simply too busy!"

3. *Foolishness*—Whenever we become consumed with what is foolish and trivial, we will fail to pray. It's a given! And then what happens? We begin to lose our ability to know the difference between good and evil (Hebrews 5:14), between what is wise and foolish, between the essential and meaningless. And then what happens? We lose sight of *the* primary thing in life—our relationship with God! We foolishly spend our very limited and priceless time and energy on the "wrong" and inferior things. We fail to "seek first his kingdom and his righteousness" so all the other things we need in life can be given to us (Matthew 6:33).

But, praise God, the opposite is true when we pray! God gives us wisdom—*His* wisdom! *He* helps us direct our energy, efforts, and time toward what truly matters in the big picture of life—living life as God means for it to be lived. He helps us remember that secondary things in life—comfort, security, money, fashion—come "not from the Father but from the world" and will most definitely "pass away" (1 John 2:16-17).

So pray, dear one! Commit your life to what *really* counts. Focus your life on the eternal, not the earthly! That's what the wise woman does—and it's done through prayer.

"He is no fool who gives what he cannot keep to gain what he cannot lose." —Jim Elliot

4. *Distance*—You can talk all day long with people you know really well, but you probably have difficulty talking even five minutes with a stranger. And the same thing happens in our communication with God. When you and I don't have a close enough relationship with God, we find it hard to talk to Him. So the solution is obvious—we must begin talking to God through prayer. We must "come near to God" (James 4:8).

If for *any* reason you are putting off talking to God through prayer, make a step—*now!*—to reconnect. It's urgent! Don't put it off! God hasn't changed, disappeared, or withdrawn His love for you or stopped listening to you. No, if there's a problem, it is always with you and me. So, close the gap. Draw close to God. Simply take a step in prayer! He's waiting for you.

5. *Ignorance*—We don't really understand God's goodness or His desire and ability to provide for us "immeasurably more than all we ask or imagine"

(Ephesians 3:20) and to "meet all our needs" (Philippians 4:19). Therefore, we don't ask or pray. Yet the truth is that God wants to grant our requests, to give us the desires of our hearts, and to bless us. It's His nature. God is good, my friend! And God is a giving God (James 1:5). But God also wants us to ask.

> ❀ *Call to Me* and I will answer you and tell you great and unsearchable things you do not know (Jeremiah 33:3).

> ❀ *Ask* and it will be given to you...for everyone who asks receives (Matthew 7:7-8).

Dear one, answer God's call to pray and start asking! Ask boldly and passionately for the salvation of your family and friends (James 5:16). Ask earnestly for God's will as you make decisions (Acts 9:6). Ask for your daily needs at home, at school, at your job, and with your friends (Matthew 6:11). Cultivate the childlike faith of the little boy who, ready for bed, came in to announce to his family in the living room, "I'm going to say my prayers now. Anybody want anything?"

6. *Sinfulness*—We don't pray because we know we have sinned against our holy God. Adam and Eve hid themselves from God after they sinned (Genesis 3:8). And King David ceased praying and "kept silent" after he sinned (Psalm 32:3).

So what is the solution to our sinfulness? King David says, "Confess [your] transgressions to the LORD" (Psalm 32:5). James says, "Confess your sins" (James 5:16). John says also to "confess our sins" (1 John 1:9). And Jesus says to pray to God, asking Him to "forgive us" the wrongs we have done (Matthew 6:12). And then what happens? The floodgates of communion with God are again opened. As David put it, he was once again "clean...whiter than snow." And he experienced fresh and renewed joy (see Psalm 51:7-12).

So, as women who are called to prayer, we must not deny our sin, blame others for it, hide it, or excuse it. Instead, do as David did. He declared to God in his brokenness, "Against you, you only, have I sinned and done what is evil in your sight" (Psalm 51:4).

Oh, please! Don't forfeit your ability and your opportunity to pray for yourself, your family and friends, and those in need because of being too proud or stubborn to deal with sin! Too much is at stake—and at risk—to hold on to secret or "favorite" sins. Keep short accounts with God. Deal with any sin as it comes up—on the spot!—at the exact minute that you slip up and fail!

Remember, "the prayer of a *righteous* [woman] is powerful and effective" (James 5:16). In other words, the prayer of a godly woman—the one who seeks to walk in obedience, who confesses and forsakes sin (Proverbs 28:13)—brings powerful results.

7. *Faithlessness*—We don't really believe in the power of prayer. We don't think prayer makes any difference...therefore we don't pray. And yet our Lord taught that when you and I ask according to His will, "if you believe, you will receive whatever you ask for in prayer" (Matthew 21:22). If you are running low in faith, do as Jesus' disciples did. Ask God to "increase" your faith (Luke 17:5)!

8. *Pridefulness*—Prayer reflects our dependence on God. When we fail to pray, we are saying that we don't have any needs...or worse, we are saying, "God, I'll take care of it myself, thank You!" However, God calls out, "If my people who are called by my name, will humble themselves and pray and seek my face and turn from their wicked ways, then will I hear from heaven" (2 Chronicles 7:14).

   So let's be quick to humble ourselves—to bow both heart and knee—and pray to God. Let's pray as David did: "Search me, O God...see if there is any offensive way in me" (Psalm 139:23-24). Let's enjoy the blessings that come from a humble heart.

   > "The LORD is close to the brokenhearted" (Psalm 34:18).

9. *Inexperience*—We don't pray because...we don't pray! And because we don't pray, we don't know how to pray...so we don't pray! It's a vicious cycle. Yet prayer, like any skill, becomes easier when repeated. The more we pray, the more we know

how to pray. And the more we know how to pray, the more we pray. It's as simple as that.

And in case you're feeling like you are the only person who ever lived who's had difficulty praying, I want to quickly tell you that you're not! Even those closest to Jesus—His disciples—had the same problem. They watched Jesus pray. They heard Jesus pray. They even heard Jesus pray for them! Finally they went to the Master Pray-er Himself and asked, "Lord, teach us to pray" (Luke 11:1).

Pray this same prayer for yourself, dear younger sister. Pray, "Lord, teach *me* to pray!" But also take the first step and start praying...and keep praying, even when you don't feel like it, even when you think it doesn't make any difference, even if you don't know what you are doing or fear you are doing it badly. Pray! Break the cycle!

> "It is sheer nonsense to imagine we can learn the high art of communing with the Lord without setting aside time for it."[2]

10. *Laziness*—We admit that the nine obstacles to a powerful prayer life that we've discussed so far are prayer killers. But even if we overcome these nine reasons for not praying, this tenth one—laziness—will make or break us in the Prayer Department!

We've both been there and done that when it comes to laziness, right? I know I had to break some bad habits that were robbing me of the time I needed to become a woman of prayer. Two simple acts helped me move forward in beating laziness...and they still work. Take them yourself!

First is my principle of "Head for bed." As soon as dinner is over I start getting ready for bed. I finish my work (for you that's homework), wash my face and brush my teeth, check my schedule for the next day and begin a "to-do" list for tomorrow, and then get into my pj's. Then I set out my prayer notebook and Bible in the place where I will (Lord willing!) have my devotions the next morning. You see, I'm on a mission—to get to bed as early as possible...so I can get up in the morning, as early as possible, and meet with God.

Second is my principle of "Something is better than nothing." I had to stop looking for the "sweet hour of prayer" and try for something more realistic. I started with "a sweet five minutes of prayer." Then, in time, as I began to taste the fruits of time spent in prayer, I graduated, little by little, to greater lengths of time spent on bended knee.

My Checklist for Prayer

✓ *Check your heart*—Check your daily input. And check your environment. What...or who...is influencing you? And is it influencing you positively for the things of God?

I know that as a young Christian I had to turn my back on some of the most popular women's magazines. The more I read my Bible and prayed, the more I realized those magazines were feeding me a steady diet of worldliness. Sure there was some practical help there. But overall, the messages were the exact opposite of the messages God's Word was sending to my heart.

Now, how can you "turn your eyes upon Jesus" so that the things of this world will grow steadily more dim? Identify three things you can do to turn your back on the world and your heart toward spiritual things—toward God.

✓ *Check your relationship with God*—Ask yourself, "Am I praying regularly?" If your answer is *yes,* praise God…and continue on in your faithfulness. However, if your answer is *no,* ask "Why? What happened?" Then run through the list of reasons on the next page and circle the culprit that is robbing you of tending to your relationship and friendship with God. Identify the Number One excuse you are allowing to keep you from prayer.

neglect	bitterness
laziness	putting it off
sin	other interests
pride	other reasons

I'm sure you know the next step: Stop right now, bow your head and your heart before God, admit your failure to pray...and then pray, even if just for five minutes. Or, put another way, what excuses have you been using for neglecting to pray? Remember, God is waiting for you! What would you like to talk over and settle with Him now?

✓   *Check your desire*—In almost every TV or radio interview I take part in concerning prayer, I'm usually asked to share one step a woman can take right away to begin making prayer a reality in her life. And my answer is always the same—"She must desire it!" Dear one, all said and done, we must desire to pray, desire to be women of prayer, desire to answer God's call to pray.

You see, you and I can know we need to pray, and we can learn the skills involved in praying. Yet, if we never desire to pray, our knowledge and skills mean nothing. Praying will never become a habit or a discipline if the one main ingredient—desire!—is missing. How do you rate your Desire Quotient?

None at all?   So-so?

Getting there?   Red hot?

How could you increase the level of your desire to pray? What do you think would help?

✎ Answering God's Call to You

We've spent a great deal of time, space, and effort looking at the reasons you and I don't pray. So now we wonder, *How does a woman after God's own heart (that's you!) answer God's high calling to pray?* Believe it or not, it's not as difficult as you think. Once you begin to tend to your heart and to the issues that keep you from praying...

Prayer is so simple;
It is like quietly opening a door
And slipping into the very presence of God,
There is the stillness
To listen to His voice;
Perhaps to petition,
Or only to listen:
It matters not.
Just to be there
In His presence
Is prayer.[3]

Now, won't you slip into the very presence of God? He's waiting for you to talk with Him about your life.

Would You Like to Know More?
Check It Out!

Read 1 John 2:15-17. How does the world tempt us? What will ultimately happen to the things of the world?

How did Jesus say to handle the temptations the world throws at you (Matthew 26:41)?

Read Luke 10:38-42. What do you see these two sisters doing that was good? What problem did Martha have? What did Jesus say to her? What did Jesus say about Mary? How can you make the same choice Mary made?

Read Psalm 32:1-5. What happens when you don't confess your sin to God? What happens when you do? What does 1 John 1:9 say happens when you do?

Read Luke 11:1-4. What was the scene in verse 1? How did Jesus answer His disciples? What do you like most about "The Lord's Prayer"? What can you add to your prayers from Jesus' model prayer?

My List of Things I Don't Want to Forget...
...from This Chapter

Praying
from the
Heart

When You Are in Trouble or in Need...Pray!

What is prayer? Referring to prayer as "the pathway to the heart of God," my friend and author Terry Glaspey writes,

> To ask the question, "What is prayer?"...probes not only the mysteries of what it means to be a human being, but even inquires into the mystery of God Himself.... Because it is a topic too deep for the human intellect, it requires that we look to God as our teacher.[1]

And this, my young praying friend, is exactly what you and I must do right now! We must look to God's Word—the Bible—for *God's* definition of prayer. At the same time we must not forget that prayer is a part of "the mystery of God Himself." That means we will never completely understand it.

Think of prayer as being like a gem with many facets carved into it, each one being beautiful and brilliant, making the gem truly magnificent. In this chapter we'll examine two of prayer's exciting facets, two slightly different kinds of prayer.

In Times of Trouble...Pray!

First of all, when you are in trouble you are to pray. And by "trouble" I don't mean when you've done something wrong. (We'll deal with that later.) No, this is the kind of prayer for those times when you have a big problem and desperately need God's intervention.

That's when we ask God for help. As Philippians 4:6 tells us, "Do not be anxious about anything, but in everything, by prayer and petition, with thanksgiving, present your requests to God." Clearly we are to cry "*Help!*" when we are troubled by someone, something...or anything! We are to go to *God* and pray to *Him* for help with our needs...like the young woman Esther did.

Queen Esther faced trouble—Queen Esther's story is told in the book of the Bible called Esther. And when the beautiful Esther faced trouble, she went to God and talked things over with Him. Here's what happened...

In order to save the lives of God's people, Queen Esther had to risk her life by approaching her husband, the king. However, coming uninvited into the presence of the king was punishable by death...and Esther hadn't been called for. Therefore, Esther fasted for three days and nights before she acted. Then, and only then, did Esther humbly draw near to the only person who could possibly help her and her people (the Jews). The Scriptures report that Esther went to the king to beg for mercy and plead with him for her people."

And the end of the story? God went to work in the shadows of the night and set in motion a fantastic series of events that led to the salvation of His people!

King Hezekiah faced trouble—Hezekiah, king of Judah, also prayed to God in a time of great trouble. Briefly, Sennacherib, ruler of Assyria, sent a letter to King Hezekiah threatening him and putting down "the living God."

What did the king do? Hezekiah took the letter, "spread it out before the LORD," and asked for God's help. He pleaded, "O LORD our God, deliver us from his hand" (2 Kings 19:19).

And the end of the story? The answer to Hezekiah's prayers to God for help? God Himself said, "*I* will defend this city and save it" (verse 34).

And we can't stop there! Oh, no! The next verse reports, "That night the angel of the LORD went out and put to death a hundred and eighty-five thousand men in the Assyrian camp. When the people got up the next morning—there were all the dead bodies!" (verse 35).

Now, *that's* an answer to prayer!

Jesus spoke of trouble—Jesus also tells us to pray in times of trouble. He "told His disciples a parable...that they should always pray and not give up" (Luke 18:1). Praying instead of giving up means looking to God in times of trouble. This kind of praying keeps us from caving in.

And what causes a cave-in? Weakness on one side and pressure on another. When the going gets rough, we are not to faint, lose heart, give in, give up, and cave in. Instead we are to pray to God, trust God, and move forward.

> "He who kneels most stands best."
> —D.L. MOODY

Dear heart, in times of trouble...pray! You can always pray in helplessness, when you can't do anything else. So put your prayer-weapon to good use in your times of trouble.

I once read a story about a young boy who was saved from drowning by his brother and carried home unconscious by his group of friends. The grateful father wanted to know exactly who had done what so he could properly thank each child. So he said to John...

"Well, John, what did you do?" He replied, "Oh, I jumped into the water and pulled him out!"

"And James and Thomas, what did you do?" questioned the dad.

"Oh, we carried Danny home!"

"And Mary, what did you do?" came the next inquiry.

And poor little Mary, who was only three years old, burst into tears and said, "Daddy, I couldn't do anything at all, so I just prayed and prayed!"

Then her father gently said, "Mary, you deserve the most praise of all, for you did all you could, and God answered your prayers through John and James and Thomas."

My friend, in times of trouble...when you can't do anything at all...just pray and pray! Turn to God in prayer during the tough times, when you don't know where else to go or what else to do.

In Times of Need...Pray!

I'm sure you're like me—you have an extremely l-o-n-g list of things you need to talk over with God—issues, school problems, people problems, parent problems, boy- or girlfriend problems, loneliness problems. As you and I well know, we encounter trouble daily. Plus we get hurt by others. And we can become overwhelmed by the stresses and pains of life. Add to this list our doubts and worries about ourselves and our lives, and it's easy to see our tremendous need for prayer!

So what can we do? This next facet in God's jewel of prayer gives us instruction regarding the personal needs of our hearts and lives as God's women: In times of need... pray!

Think again about Philippians 4:6. Here God tells us that "in everything, by prayer and petition, with thanksgiving, present your requests to God." We are told to "pray in the Spirit on all occasions with all kinds of prayers and requests" (Ephesians 6:18). In other words, there is something you can—and should!—do about the pressing needs in your life, your family, your friendships, your schooling, your job, and your everyday life: You are to pray to God about your *specific* needs—to talk over the *specific* needs in your life with Him, with the God of the universe! For instance,

 Jesus told His followers to pray for their enemies, for those who hurt them (Matthew 5:44).

 Jesus also taught His disciples to pray regarding their need for food each day (Matthew 6:11).

 Paul asked others to pray for him to have opportunities to share the gospel of Jesus Christ (Colossians 4:3).

 Paul prayed for the Philippian believers, for his friend Timothy, and for the salvation of his countrymen (Philippians 1:1-4; 1 Timothy 2:1-6).

 Jesus prayed about His death (Matthew 26:36-46).

Our Savior and these saints of old prayed for specific needs, desires, problems, and requests. And we are to do the same. We must lift up the daily details and the personal needs in our lives to God through specific prayer requests. What kind of needs?

Health and energy—This is first on my list! God has given us hefty job assignments as Christian women. Our to-do lists are long...and so are our days! Therefore, we need to pray for energy and endurance, for focus and staying power so we can continue moving toward the goal of getting our work done, whether that's our housework, homework, or work on a job.

Attitude—Place this one near the top of your prayer list! Pray for a joyful spirit, patience with any obstacles...or people-problems...that come up during your day. And pray for self-control so emotions don't spill out and hurt someone else (Galatians 5:22-23).

Faithfulness—Pray, too, to keep your eyes—and heart!—fixed on the end of the day so that you will continue pressing and reaching to its very end. Pray to finish fully on your projects. When you would dearly love to be doing something else but you need to go to practice, finish your school work, help your mom with the housework, help your dad with yard work, or help out with your younger brother or sister, pray to be "trustworthy in everything" (1 Timothy 3:11).

Work—My "work" is probably different than yours. (It's more like your homework—I have to turn in my writing on due dates!) But if you have a job babysitting or working part-time somewhere, then your prayers should include your workplace, your workmates, and your faithfulness on the job. Pray to work willingly and eagerly with your heart and hands "as to the Lord" (Proverbs 31:13 and Colossians 3:23).

Wisdom—And every woman, whatever her age, needs God's wisdom with decision-making! So we must ask for it: "If any of you lacks wisdom, he should ask God...and it will be given to him" (James 1:5).

Relationships—All women—whether younger or older— have relationships with parents and family members that need to be prayed over. There are also friendships and a desire for companionship (both male and female!) that need to be talked over with God. We must pray, as Romans 12:18 says, to "live at peace with everyone."

> "Prayer perfumes every relationship."

Well, I'm sure you realize that on and on...and longer and longer...the list of our prayer needs grows! And the balm to our hurting hearts and consuming needs is to answer God's call to prayer and *pray*! So give your stressful concerns—each and every one of them—to your all-wise, all-powerful, and all-gracious God. Only by praying always in the Spirit will we keep in the eye of the storm. Only then...and there...will we know "the peace of God, which transcends all understanding" (Philippians 4:7).

Now, let the prayers begin! Don't get bogged down under a load of heavy concerns about your daily life. Pray instead! "In *everything,* by prayer and petition...present your requests to God." Let your prayers ascend! Send your heart-cries to God every day as you pray minute-by-minute, step-by-step, and word-by-word.

My Checklist for Prayer

✓ *Look for trouble*—Does this sound strange? We must always remember that trouble is part of the Christian life. It's something we must accept as a fact of life. It helped me tremendously to underline the little word "whenever" in James 1:2: "Consider it pure joy, my brothers, whenever you face trials of many kinds." As he wrote about trials in life, James did not say *if...*but he said *whenever.* The apostle Peter also wrote of the fact of trials and troubles. He urged us, "Dear friends, do not be surprised at the painful trial you are suffering, as though something strange were happening to you" (1 Peter 4:12).

You and I, dear one, must face life with our eyes wide open! We must accept the fact of trouble. Then we must devise a plan for handling trouble and for dealing with it—God's way. For instance, what will you think when trouble arrives? What scriptures will you use to stay strong in the Lord as you walk through your own painful trials? And what, when, and how will you pray about the troubles of life— past, present, and future? Be prepared for trouble.

Wisdom always has a plan, so create your plan of action for facing trouble. What will it be?

✓ *Look to God in prayer daily*—Your needs arrive daily...and so do challenges and difficulties. Don't make the mistake of thinking you can meet trouble head-on, take it in stride, and enjoy victory *without* your all-powerful heavenly Father's help! Be wise and ask for help daily. It's His day, and you are His child. And "with God we will gain the victory" (Psalm 60:12).

> "Much prayer, much power."[2]

"Be strong and take heart, all you who hope in the LORD" (Psalm 31:24). You need guidance for today, and God promises to "instruct you and teach you in the way you should go" and to "watch over you" (Psalm 32:8). You need wisdom for today, and it's yours...if you will "trust in the LORD with all your heart and lean not on your own understanding" (Proverbs 3:5). You need patience for today, and patience is His specialty, one of His fruit of the Spirit (Galatians 5:22).

And the list goes on...as does God's provision for your needs! What are your special needs today? Which of the verses just mentioned encourage you, and why? Now, pray!

✓ *Look for highlights*—Trouble is a fact of life, but so are God's rich, abundant blessings! So remember to look for...and thank God for...His blessings. What kind of blessings or highlights? One highlight arrives with the sunlight each new day—"Because of the LORD's great love we are not consumed, for his compassions never fail. They are new every morning; great is your faithfulness" (Lamentations 3:22-23). Here's another—"Weeping may remain for a night, but rejoicing comes in the morning" (Psalm 30:5). So..."praise the LORD, O my soul; all my inmost being, praise his holy name...and forget not all his benefits" (Psalm 103:1-2).

What benefits has God brought your way this week? Today? Name them right here and now. That way they will be recorded and not forgotten. Then thank Him...profusely!

✎ Answering God's Call to You

Are you grasping the importance of a deep-rooted prayer-life? When you are in the habit of praying, you are more likely to pray when trouble arises. And when you are in the habit of praying, you are more likely to think of asking for God's help *first* instead of later...or last, when all else fails.

So I pray God's message to your heart is crystal clear. When you're in trouble...pray! When you're helpless... pray! When you've done all you can do but you're still in need of help...pray! When you encounter an only-God-can-meet-it need...pray! When you have a specific need... pray! Prayer is God's avenue for you. He calls you to pray whenever something—anything!—is important to you. So in times of trouble and need...pray!

Now, what change must you make to be more consistent at regular prayer? What could you do that would make all the difference in the world in your prayer-life? Think of that one thing. What difference would it make? And when can you get started? Put it on your personal prayer list, enlist the aid of another person to help you with accountability, and then go to work on kicking your efforts at prayer up a notch!

Would You Like to Know More?
Check It Out!

Read Esther 4:8-17. Note several ways Esther approached her troubles.

Read 2 Kings 19:14-19. Note several ways King Hezekiah approached his troubles.

What lessons do you want to remember from Queen Esther and King Hezekiah?

List your top five specific "needs," whether issues, attitudes, problems, or relationships.

How do the following verses encourage, comfort, or instruct you about your needs and how to deal with them?

Matthew 6:11—

Romans 12:18—

Philippians 4:6-7—

Philippians 4:19—

James 1:5—

My List of Things I Don't Want to Forget...
...from This Chapter

_____

_____

_____

_____

_____

_____

_____

_____

_____

_____

_____

_____

_____

_____

_____

_____

_____

_____

_____

_____

When You Are Disappointed or Hurting ...Pray!

I'm sure you know how it feels to be disappointed or hurt by another person. Friends and family are part of life—and both can bring us extreme joy...and sometimes extreme sorrow and pain. Like me, you've probably had some friendships that started out great, but in time something was missing or went wrong. Maybe the other person got a new best friend...or a new girlfriend. Maybe your friends said something about you that wasn't true...or that hurt you. Maybe they turned against you. Maybe they walked away from your special friendship...and joined a clique. Maybe they let you down when you were really counting on their help. And in the end you were left wondering, "What happened?"

Whatever it was, we've both been there and done that when it comes to being let down or wounded by friends and family. And when it's over, we feel confused and discouraged. So what are we to do when such frustrating and heartbreaking things happen in our relationships? What are we to do with our broken hearts? And how are we to go on afterward?

As always, God comes to our rescue. He has all of the answers for us...and prayer is one of them!

Forgive and Pray for Others

Oh, is it ever hard to forgive people who have disappointed us or failed us as friends! And if we aren't careful, we can carry a grudge toward them and allow bitterness or resentment to take root in our hearts (Hebrews 12:15). Or we can follow another natural tendency and no longer have anything to do with them. But God's Word has wisdom for us here. We are to be *"forgiving* each other, just as in Christ God forgave [us]" (Ephesians 4:32; Colossians 3:13). Jesus, too, models the right way—*His* way!—of dealing with those who disappoint us. He says we are to *pray* for them (Luke 6:28).

And so we *forgive*...and we *pray*.

Three godly men in the Bible show us God's better— no, make that best!—way to handle our pain when people—even friends and family—let us down.

When people disappoint you, look to Samuel—Samuel spent his life teaching God's law and standards to God's people. But, sadly, the day came when they rejected Samuel and his message to them. That's when God told Samuel to speak to the people about their sin. What sin had they committed? They wanted a king to lead them instead of trusting God to lead them through His prophets—prophets like Samuel!

When Samuel confronted the masses with their sin, they were ashamed and begged him to pray for them. And what was Samuel's response to their request that he pray for them, the very people who had rejected him and disobeyed God? Did he snub them? Leave them to fend for themselves? No, Samuel *forgave* God's people...and *prayed* for them. He said, "Far be it from me that I should sin against the LORD by failing to pray for you" (1 Samuel 12:23).

When family disappoints you, look to Moses—Moses prayed for his brother, Aaron, after Aaron disappointed him and God. While Moses was away, Aaron, the high priest of God and Moses' co-leader, was in charge of God's people. And he clearly disobeyed the commands of God by making a golden calf for God's people to worship (Exodus 32:8; Deuteronomy 9:12-20), and God was on the warpath!

And how mad was God at Aaron? The Bible reports that the Lord was very angry with Aaron and would have destroyed him (Deuteronomy 9:19). Aaron had had it. He was done for. It was over! There seemed to be no hope for Aaron's life. Yet Moses *forgave* his brother and *prayed* and asked God to spare the life of his sinning brother.

When friends disappoint you, look to Job—Job is described in the Bible as "blameless and upright," as one who "feared God and shunned evil" (Job 1:1). Yet Job was verbally attacked by his friends at the very same time he was enduring the loss of basically all that he had—family, health, and wealth.

How did Job handle his friends' criticism? How did he respond to their lack of understanding and their failure to help in his time of need? Job was patient. Job was humble.

And, finally, it was God Himself who stepped in and put an end to Job's friends' wrong accusations and guesses about why Job was suffering.

Yet Job, after receiving much criticism from these close companions, prayed for his friends. In fact, God sent the sinning trio of friends *to* Job, saying, "Go to my servant Job. …My servant Job will pray for you, and I will accept his prayer and not deal with you according to your folly" (Job 42:8). And the righteous Job *forgave* his friends and *prayed* for them.

Watch Your Heart!

Samuel forgave God's people…and prayed for them. Moses forgave his brother…and prayed for him. And Job forgave his critical friends…and prayed for them. And that's what you and I need to do. How is this possible? It is possible when you watch over your heart. As Psalm 66:18 explains regarding prayer, "If I had cherished sin in my heart, the Lord would not have listened." And, as Proverbs 28:9 states, "If anyone turns a deaf ear to the law, even his prayers are detestable."

> "We must forgive others so we can pray for them."

If we fail to forgive others, we are failing to obey God. That means our hearts are no longer pure, and our prayers become repulsive to God. Then we are unable to pray for others…due to our sin of failing to forgive. It's a vicious cycle—one you don't want to get into! So here's what we need to do: We must forgive others…so that our hearts are right before *God*…so that we can pray for those who sin, who fail, and who disappoint us (James 5:16).

So be careful, dear heart! Jesus says, "Love your enemies" (Matthew 5:44). When it comes to praying for others in a hurtful situation, there can be no personal accounting system of wrongs committed.

> "Love does not keep account of evil.
> Love keeps no score of wrongs."
> —1 Corinthians 13:5[1]

What should we do? Forgive others and pray to God for them—even those who disappoint and hurt us. Our heart attitude—even toward our enemies—should be like that of Samuel: "Pray for you? Yes, to my latest breath! God forbid that I should sin against the Lord in ceasing to pray for you."[2]

Offer a Helping Hand

Are you familiar with the fable that tells of a man who is crying for help while he is drowning in a river? Meanwhile, on the bridge that spans the water, another man is casually leaning over the rail looking at the struggling man. According to the story, the observer is telling the dying man what he *ought* to have done and letting him know what he *should* do if he ever gets into that situation again. Instead of reaching in with a helping hand and saving the dying man's life, he talks on and on. Clearly the perishing man didn't need a lecture. He needed help! He needed someone to save his life!

And that's what you and I have to do when it comes to praying for those who have fallen and failed. We must help them! We must set aside our disappointment, stop with the lectures, put aside judgment, and go to work helping and praying for others. Sure, correction and instruction may come later. Talking about the incident and trying to rebuild our relationships may come later. But when a person has failed and is in trouble, be sure to pray...*and* offer a helping hand!

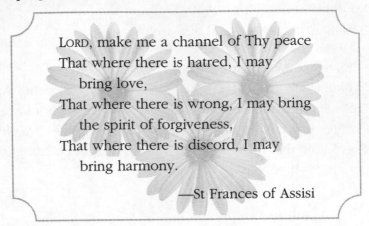

> LORD, make me a channel of Thy peace
> That where there is hatred, I may
>   bring love,
> That where there is wrong, I may bring
>   the spirit of forgiveness,
> That where there is discord, I may
>   bring harmony.
>
> —St Frances of Assisi

Help for Your Hurting Heart

Are you ready for more help for your hurting heart? Yet another facet in the treasured gem of prayer is the opportunity to fight your battles in prayer instead of against a person. When you have been harmed by someone, when your heart hurts because of betrayal or unfairness or evil, you can become a prayer-warrior.

Meet someone whose heart was hurt—Meet David, a warrior and a king—*and* a prayer-warrior! In Psalm 55, David poured out his torn and bleeding heart in a prayer and cried out to God against his enemies. David had been betrayed—by both family and friends—and he went to battle through prayer.

The background of this psalm is absolutely heartbreaking. Jerusalem, "the city of David," was taken over from David by Absalom, David's own son. To make things worse, Ahithophel, David's best friend, turned away from David to follow Absalom. The people of the city also turned against David and threw him out.

Are you someone who's been hurt?—As I'm sitting here writing at my desk, I am thinking of you, my dear younger sister. I'm wondering, *Are you someone who's been hurt?* Not one day goes by that I don't receive letters and emails from women—young and old...and everything in between—who have been hurt by others. I know firsthand that people hurt people. I also know that God's people hurt God's people. And I'm aware that family members hurt family members.

So what are we, as God's women, to do when our hearts hurt and when we've been hurt by loved ones, friends, family, by those we looked up to and respected, by those we trusted? The answer, of course, is...*pray!* And David shows us how.

Lessons on Praying from a Hurting Heart

Lesson #1—Cast your burden on the Lord. David knew *where* to turn and *what* to do. He knew to "cast [his] cares on the LORD" (Psalm 55:22).

> Listen to my prayer, O God, do not ignore my plea; hear me and answer me....My heart is in anguish within me; the terrors of death assail me (verses 1-2,4).

> "God is the very One who says to us—roll your anxieties over on Me, for I have you in My heart!"[3]

Like David, you and I have an almighty and all-loving Father to help us carry our loads.

Lesson #2—Resist the temptation to run away. David's natural desire was to leave the scene, to flee from the problem and the pain. Who wouldn't think, "No way am I going to stay here and take this. I'm out of here! I don't need this"? So David wished for wings!

> Oh, that I had the wings of a dove! I would fly away and be at rest—I would flee far away, and stay in the desert; I would hurry to my place of shelter (verses 6-8).

Beloved, when you find yourself surrounded by "enemies" or suffering because of the failure of your friends, you will most certainly wish for the wings of a dove that you might fly away and be at rest! But you must stay and fight your battle by placing your prayers into battle array. And you must pray, pray, pray!

And be assured, dear praying heart, that if "a way out" becomes necessary, if the heat of battle becomes more than you can bear, "God is faithful." He promises that *He* will provide an escape route (1 Corinthians 10:13). *He* will deliver you. *He* will come to your aid. *He* will rescue you. *He* will see to it! You can depend on *Him*. As David declared, "I call to God, and the Lord saves me....He hears my voice" (Psalm 55:16-17)!

Lesson #3—Believe that God will sustain you. David's confidence in God is powerful. He pounds out his prayers, never letting up, repeatedly hammering out the truths that God will take care of him: "The LORD saves me....He hears my voice....God...will hear [my enemies] and afflict them. ...He will never let the righteous fall" (Psalm 55:16-22). Finally, after such praying and after counting on God's promises, David shouted out his final assurance—"I trust in you" (verse 23)! His prayers have at last gotten through to his own soul. At last, David stops thinking about the enemy and turns his full focus—and trust—upon the Lord God Almighty who hears His people's pleas and saves them.

Oh, dear reading friend, when all seems hopeless, put your God-given faith to work and trust in the Lord. Believe that no matter what burden you bear, He will sustain you in it today...and all the days of your life!

My Checklist for Prayer

✓ *Check your heart*—A forgiving heart is a heart that can pray for others. And if you think you can't forgive someone, consider these truths about *your* heart: "For all have sinned and fall short of the glory of God"; "if you think you are standing firm, be careful that you don't fall"; "if we claim to be without sin, we deceive ourselves and the truth is not in us."[4]

Is there anyone you are failing to forgive? What example did Jesus set for us when He prayed on the cross, "Father, forgive them, for they do not know what they are doing" (Luke 23:34)? How can you follow His example?

✓   *Check your relationships*—Christ calls you to love
     others—even your enemies. His instructions con-
     cerning those who have wronged you come from
     Luke 6:27-28:

> *love*...your enemies,
> *do good*...to those who hate you,
> *bless*...those who curse you,
> *pray*...for those who mistreat you.

What good can you do for someone who has
harmed you or let you down? Are you speaking kind
words to and about those who have slandered or verbally attacked you? What commitment can you make
to pray for those who have hurt or disappointed you?
Look to God for His help. Then do what He leads
you to do to love your enemies.

✓   *Check your prayer-life*—When your heart hurts, that's exactly when you must seek God on bended knee. Pray! Don't allow yourself to rant, rave, dissolve into a puddle, fall apart, or collapse. Instead of giving up, pray (Luke 18:1)! And while you are praying, cast your cares and burdens upon the Lord (Psalm 55:22).

With God's help and with much prayer, go on with life...silently, cheerfully, in the power and grace of the Holy Spirit (Galatians 5:22-23). Go on, knowing that God is still on His throne. He is still in control, He is still sovereign, He is still all-powerful, and He is still able...and He always will be! And He will deal with those who harm His children (Psalm 37:7-9). He promises it!

What was your reaction the last time you were disappointed or hurt by someone? The next time someone lets you down or is cruel to you, what better response (by God's grace!) would you like to give? How can prayer help?

✎ Answering God's Call to You

What happens when you turn to God and answer His call to prayer during your times of distress and pain? God sweetens what is bitter (Exodus 15:23-25). He makes the one who is sad become glad (Psalm 30:11). And He turns something bad into something good (Romans 8:28). Oh, please, don't wish your hard times away! Some of your most meaningful times with God will come when you talk to Him about your hurting heart. So fly away in prayer... and rest in Him!

Now, what is troubling you, my precious reading friend? I'm praying here at my desk for you as you face your challenges. I'm praying that in your times of trouble you never forget to pray to your almighty, all-powerful, miracle-working, mountain-moving God! Don't just stand there! Don't cave in! Don't worry! And don't suffer! "Is any one among you in trouble? He should *pray*" (James 5:13).

What a Friend We Have in Jesus

What a Friend we have in Jesus,
All our sins and griefs to bear!
What a privilege to carry
Ev'rything to God in prayer!
O what peace we often forfeit,
O what needless pain we bear,
All because we do not carry
Ev'rything to God in prayer!

Have we trials and temptations?
Is there trouble anywhere?
We should never be discouraged—
Take it to the Lord in prayer.
Can we find a friend so faithful
Who will all our sorrows share?
Jesus knows our ev'ry weakness—
Take it to the Lord in prayer.

Are we weak and heavy laden,
Cumbered with a load of care?
Precious Savior, still our refuge—
Take it to the Lord in prayer.
Do thy friends despise, forsake thee?
Take it to the Lord in prayer;
In His arms He'll take and shield thee—
Thou wilt find a solace there.[5]

Would You Like to Know More?
Check It Out!

What do these verses say you should do when someone disappoints or hurts you?

Ephesians 4:32—

Colossians 3:13—

Luke 6:27-28—

1 Corinthians 13:5—

What should your attitude be when others fail?

Proverbs 24:17-18—

1 Corinthians 10:12—

Galatians 6:1-2—

What do these verses teach you about suffering?

John 16:33—

2 Timothy 2:12—

James 1:2—

1 Peter 1:6—

What does God say to do when you are suffering?

Psalm 55:22—

1 Peter 5:7—

My List of Things I Don't Want to Forget...
...from This Chapter

When You Are Worried or Overwhelmed... Pray!

Would you like to meet a first-class worrier? Well, check that off your goal list. You have...and it's me! In fact, I should write a book entitled *Confessions of a Worrywart*. But until then, believe me, I've seen the inside of a doctor's office more than a few times. You name it—a bleeding ulcer, colitis, and eczema up to my elbows—I've been there. And I know I'm not alone. Women of all ages love to worry... about anything and everything!

What do we worry about most?

About our relationships with our parents, brothers and sisters, friends and acquaintances. And we can't stop there! Oh no, we've also got to worry about relationships with our enemies—about knowing what to do and how to handle these problems!

Then there are other items on "The Great List of Things to Worry About." These include worrying about what others think of us, what we look like—if we are too fat or too thin, if we are pretty enough. And don't leave out worrying about health, safety, finances for schooling, boyfriends, dating, the future...nicely topped off with worrying about our school-work, exams, and grades, about getting up in front of others, about an upcoming social event.

And here's another big area! My husband and I were in New York City the day of the September 11, 2001, World Trade Center collapse. That terrorist attack came just six hours after we welcomed my daughter Katherine's little baby Matthew into this world...in the very hospital that became the burn unit for the victims of the disaster that day. Many New Yorkers continue to worry about another terrorist attack...as do most of us.

And we worry about war.

On and on the list of worries goes. And yet...

God Commands Us, "Do Not Worry!"

Did you know that over 300 times in the New Testament God commands us to not worry or be anxious? Just one of these times is Philippians 4:6-7:

> Do not be anxious about anything, but in everything by prayer and petition, with thanksgiving, present your requests to God. And the peace of God, which transcends all understanding, will guard your hearts and minds in Christ Jesus.

Beloved, these are the verses that finally knocked some sense into me about my worrying habit and its devastating effects. They spoke so clearly to my fretting heart that I wrote the verses out on a card and memorized them. I reviewed these scriptures and recited them over and over. I never went anywhere without my memory card. I carried

God's command with me—physically on the card and spiritually in my heart—and took it apart word-by-word.

And sure enough, just like God's active and powerful Word always does, it began to change my heart and mind (Hebrews 4:12)! I went from worrying to worshiping. Instead of fretting, I began to trust the God of the promise. Here's what I discovered.

> "Trust in the LORD with all your heart" (Proverbs 3:5).

The command—"Do not be anxious about anything." God's Word clearly instructs us to take care of our responsibilities and relationships and daily life. But beyond that, we are not to worry...about anything...ever...period! In the book of Philippians, where this medicine for worriers is found, we meet some people who had a lot of causes for worry.

First of all, the Philippians themselves had *people* problems—they had enemies who stood against them in their battle for the faith of the gospel (Philippians 1:27-28). As a result, they had potential *emotional* problems—their joy in the Lord was at risk (3:1). And they had potential *spiritual* problems—their strength for the battle was in danger (4:1).

Then there was Paul, the man who is writing this advice to the Philippians. Talk about problems! Paul was in prison...waiting to see if he would live or die! On top of his stressful situation, Paul also suffered from some kind of physical or personal "thorn in the flesh" (2 Corinthians 12:7). Writing from his own problem-ridden life, Paul shared this command with his friends in Philippi...and with you and me:

Do not be anxious about anything.

These six words make it plain that, for the Christian, all worry is forbidden by God. And that's that!

The scope of the command—"Do not be anxious *about anything.*" Take your pen in hand and circle the words "about anything" in the six words above. The New King James version translates the first part of Philippians 4:6: "Be anxious for nothing." And what is "nothing"? I once heard a Bible teacher say, "*Nothing* is a zero with the rim kicked off!" And that's God's message to our hearts. When it comes to worrying, we are to be anxious "for nothing." There aren't many other words beyond *nothing* and *anything* to use to describe the scope of God's command!

Are you wondering, *Yes, I get it...but how do I not worry?* Well, take heart! God has the answer to all your problems...

The solution—Prayer! "Present your requests to God." Yes, life is difficult, full of problems and filled with stress. And yes, worry is a natural tendency. And, praise God, yes, there is something we can do to keep from worrying! And yes, we *can* obey God's command to "not be anxious about anything." God's solution is this: When you are worried...pray! Pray *from* your heart and *with all* your heart! Pray, pray, pray!

And like the colors in the arch of a rainbow across the sky, God gives us several brilliant ways to win over worry. Instead of worrying about *any*thing, He says, "in *every*thing...present your requests to God." How?

By prayer—Prayer is worship, but it's also where all true worship begins...and all worry ends!

 By petition—Do you have a need, a concern? Then pray! Boldly go before God's throne of grace in your times of need...and with your needs (Hebrews 4:16). Don't fail to shoot your prayers heavenward and ask the all-powerful, almighty God of the universe. He can solve all your problems! You see, we can either ask and not worry... or we can worry because we don't ask. It's one or the other—and the choice is ours.

 With thanksgiving—A thankful heart that focuses on God's sovereign power over everything and on His purposes in everything cannot be a worrying heart. Neither can a heart of trust, a heart that is at rest. So give God thanks now. Thank Him profusely!

 By requests—"Present your requests to God" with utmost trust. Keep nothing back, great or small. Withhold nothing—none of your concerns—from God. He wants your *every* concern! So present them to Him. Leave them in the lap of the Almighty.

The result—And then what happens? "The peace of God" comes to our rescue. It "will guard [our] hearts and [our] minds in Christ Jesus." In other words, as a tribal missionary so beautifully and simply translated this truth, "Jesus will make your heart sit down."

And once your heart sits down, peace keeps watch over it. Like a soldier, God's peace guards your heart—and mind!—against fear, worry, stress, and fretting. And the result? The battle against worry is won.

❀ ❀ ❀

But there's another life situation that is far beyond worry, and that is when you are overwhelmed. I'm sure you've been shaken to the core at some time in your life by a serious, earth-shattering, almost overwhelming crisis. A time when you felt crushed. A time when you believed you could not go on...or weren't sure how to go on. Unfortunately, pain and sorrow, loss and tragedy, confusion and frustration touch every life. It's just as Jesus warned us, "In this world you will have trouble" (John 16:33). It's terrible, isn't it?

If terrible trials are a fact of life, what can we do when we go through such experiences? Answer: We can go straight to God because He has a set of instructions for making life work when it seems like it will never work again. God has given us two—yes, two!—glorious resources for dealing with a crushing situation.

First, when we are overwhelmed, we have the Bible, God's guidebook for handling all of life and its every problem (2 Peter 1:3).

And second...

God Helps Us to Pray

Through the act of prayer you and I can seek the heart and mind of God *in* our difficult situations. That's because God gives us help for answering His call to prayer. He gives us this assurance for our difficult times:

> In the same way, the Spirit helps us in our weakness. We do not know what we ought to pray for, but the Spirit himself intercedes for us with groans that words cannot express....The Spirit intercedes for the saints in accordance with God's will (Romans 8:26-27).

Here we discover that God Himself gives us help and hope in our impossible situations. The Holy Spirit literally comes to our rescue as He "happens" upon us in our trouble. He lends us His helping hand by praying and pleading to God on our behalf, with "groans" and sighs that baffle words. It is supernatural, so we cannot understand it. But in simple language, the Holy Spirit groans and sighs *for* us in prayer.

What good news! When you don't know what to pray for, how to pray, or what words to use, the Holy Spirit does! And He takes over and expresses our requests to God *for* us. The Spirit takes over for us and appeals to the only person who can help us—God Himself.

Thank God that you are not left alone to cope with your problems! That's the way it is for you (and me, too) when you are in overwhelming pain and sorrow. The Holy Spirit intercedes. Sometimes you are suffering personally from physical or emotional distress. At other times you pray for hurting parents or for a wounded brother or sister. You also reach toward God when there's been a loss, a tragedy, a trauma, an attack, an accident. You know you should pray. You want to pray. You try to pray. You search for the words to tell God all about your broken heart...but find none.

But take heart! When your heart is so sorrowful and bewildered that you don't even know how to pray or what to say to God, again, the Holy Spirit takes over for you.

A word for you—Again I say to you, "Thank God!" Thank Him that He knows your weaknesses, that He knows your heart, that He knows your suffering, that He knows your desire, and that He knows your need to pray. He also knows when you cannot pray, so *He*—through His Holy Spirit—comes to your rescue and prays for you!

Now, what exactly can—and should—you do when you run up against an overwhelming adversity?

My Checklist for Prayer

✓   *Don't...*miss a day of prayer—If you play hit-and-miss with your daily prayer time, you will most certainly discover that your worry level is higher on the days when you don't pray. Prayer is God's surefire solution for eliminating worry. *If* you pray, *then* you won't be anxious. *If* you pray, *then* you will experience peace of mind. And the opposite is true, too. If you *don't* pray, you will be anxious. If you *don't* pray, you will not experience peace of mind.

So...be faithful to pray. Talk with God about your life...instead of worrying about it. What are the issues that tempt you to worry? Write them in a special place—in your journal or notebook. Be sure you are recording your faithfulness in prayer on your "My Prayer Calendar" (see pages 198-99). Also record any changes in your level of concern in these areas as you pray about them.

✓ *Do...*determine a "worry day"—I can't resist passing on this fun—and funny!—practical solution for those times you think you just *have* to worry about *some-*thing!

A man who was unable to put his troubles aside completely came up with his own solution. He decided that the best thing to do would be to set apart a single day, Wednesday, to do all his worrying. When something came up that disturbed him during the week, he wrote it down and put it in his "Wednesday Worry Box."

When the time came to review his high-anxiety problems, he found to his great surprise that most of them had already been settled. There was no longer any need for worry! He discovered that most worry is unnecessary and a waste of precious energy.[2]

I know you are praying—that was part of the first check-mark activity. But if you can't resist a good round of worrying, what day will you pick as your "worry day"? Just be sure you *wait* until that day to worry! Also be sure and to record what happened to your concern during the week.

✓   *Do...*your best—Sometimes your heart cries out, "It hurts so much! It's so bad, I don't think I can pray!" What are you to do when this happens? First, remember such feelings are okay! They are normal. They are *common* (1 Corinthians 10:13). This happens to everyone. Then begin to pray. That's your part. God's part is to "join in and help" you pray.[3] He will perfect your fumbling attempts to do the right thing—to pray even when your heart hurts so badly that you are not sure what to pray or how to pray.

What is your agonizing prayer concern? And what can you do to begin to pray? Can you at least kneel down? Can you try to pray in the ways you normally do? Adore and worship God now for who He is and for what He has done for you and His people. Go ahead and thank Him for His goodness. Also acknowledge any known sin. And pray for others. Then record what happened.

✎ Answering God's Call to You

How encouraging it is to know that, as a believer, you are not left on your own to cope with life's problems. Even when you don't know the right words to pray, the Holy Spirit does...and He prays with you and for you.

My prayer for you at this moment is that you will let the prayers of your heart flow. When you are in pain...pray! When you are speechless...pray! When you are heartsick...pray! When you are suffering, beaten up, or beaten down by life...pray! When you are troubled or perplexed...pray! When you are overwhelmed...pray! Your heavenly Father knows what you need before you ask (Matthew 6:32)...so don't be afraid to bring up anything and everything. God wants to hear from you. Use any fumbling words or wails you can muster up out of your hurting heart. Just be sure you pray...and leave the rest to God.

Would You Like to Know More?
Check It Out!

God's solution to your tendency to worry is simple: Pray! Copy Philippians 4:6-7 here. Then write out what the following verses teach you about prayer.

1 Peter 5:7—

Hebrews 4:16—

How do you think praying faithfully about your problems helps to counteract worry?

Read Romans 8:26-34 in your Bible. In what ways does the Holy Spirit help believers according to...

...verse 26?

...verse 27?

What do you learn about God in verse 31?

What do you learn about Jesus Christ in verse 34?

How should these truths help you when you are worried or overwhelmed?

My List of Things I Don't Want to Forget...
...from This Chapter

Finding God's Will Through Prayer

When You Must Make a Decision...Pray for Faith and Wisdom!

I'm sure you've had a few wake-up calls in your life. (And I don't mean from your alarm clock!) Well, believe me, that happened to me one morning when a woman called to invite me to speak at her church. As she talked, my fingers drummed the table and my mind anxiously wondered, *When is she going to pause long enough for me to blurt out, "Sure! I'll come! When do you want me? I can come right now!"*

When this gracious lady was done, I breathlessly assured her I would be delighted to come to her event and went on with my day.

At about eight o'clock that night, the phone rang again. It was another sweet woman asking me to come speak at her church. As she described the event, I was shaking my head from side to side and already answering her in my mind, *No way! No how! No ma'am!* No, I didn't say these words, but they were in my heart.

The next day during my prayer time, I sat before the Lord and wondered, *Why my split responses? Each caller was a*

godly woman. Each invitation had to do with spiritual min-
istry. And each event was a wonderful opportunity for min-
istry. What had happened?

As I thought and prayed, I realized that I wasn't making
spiritual decisions. No, I was making *physical* decisions!
And suddenly it all made sense. If I felt good, the answer
was *yes!* And if I didn't feel good or was tired, well, the
answer was *No way! No how! No ma'am!*

No Decision Made without Prayer!

Once God pointed out my problem, His Word—and
example after example of Bible heroes—came rushing in
to show me the right way to make decisions.

- ❀ King Solomon prayed for wisdom...and rose up
  from prayer to become the wisest man who ever
  lived (1 Kings 3:5-12).

- ❀ Nehemiah spent time praying "before the God of
  heaven" after hearing bad news...and rose up
  knowing what action to take (Nehemiah 1:4-11).

- ❀ Queen Esther fasted three days and nights to prepare to follow God's will in a life-threatening situation (Esther 4:16)...and rose up to boldly make
  her request to the king.

- ❀ King David was a man who prayed...and became
  a man after God's own heart who fulfilled God's
  will (Acts 13:22).

- ❀ The Lord Jesus sought His Father's direction
  through prayer and rose up...declaring, "Let us go

somewhere else—to the nearby villages—so I can preach there also. That is why I have come" (Mark 1:35-39).

Right there and then, dear friend, I made a new prayer commitment: "From now on, *No decision made without prayer!*" To seal my commitment, I turned to a blank page in my prayer notebook and wrote across the top, "Decisions to Make." This prayer principle of *No decision made without prayer* has guided my life and helped me find God's

> "Out of the will of God there is no such thing as success; in the will of God there cannot be any failure."[1]

will from that day on. And it can guide yours, too.

How does passing your decision-making process through the fire of prayer help? Read on!

You Are Called to a Life of Faith

What's a busy woman to do about all of the opportunities, invitations, and decisions that come her way? And how can she know which things are God's will for her and which are not? Here's a principle from God's Word that will help guide you into a life marked by strong, powerful, confident faith. It's a guideline for making decisions and handling the doubtful things or "gray areas" of daily life:

> But the man who has doubts is condemned if he eats, because his eating is not from faith; and everything that does not come from faith is sin (Romans 14:23).

This verse has to do with violating your conscience. In general, it tells you how to know when to move ahead in full faith...and when to hold back because faith, confidence, and a clear conscience are missing. The apostle Paul is saying that if we doubt something in our hearts, or we are not sure if an action is right or wrong, then we should not do it—whatever "it" is. Doing it would be sin for us because it would cause guilt and violate our consciences. (And just a note: In the case of the Romans Paul is writing to, "it" was eating food that was forbidden in the Old Testament.)

Exactly how does this principle of doubtful things and gray areas apply to your decision-making? How does it help you live a life of faith and confidence?

1. *You are called to act in confidence*—You (and all Christians) should be sure and confident that you are doing the right thing in your actions and decisions. This kind of confidence adds unbelievable power to your life. Instead of waffling and wavering and wondering, you can act decisively and without worry.

   However, as you well know, whenever you do something that you are not sure is right or wrong, doubt sets in and takes over, weakening your confidence and bringing on guilt.

   > "Living without faith is like driving in the fog."

2. *You are called to pray for confidence*—Your goal is to live and act with the belief that what you are doing is right. Therefore, you must pray. With this goal and purpose in mind, I personally try not to

make a move or commit myself to *anything* until after prayer, which includes listening for God's response. That may take a day...or months. But what we are looking for is clear direction, a clear conscience, and the absence of doubt and guilt.

3. *You are called to peace of mind*—When you pray— and *wait* for God's answer and direction!—you will at last sense His clear direction. How will you know? Doubts will vanish, and your confidence in God's guidance will soar. When this happens to me after I've prayed (for however long it takes), I can commit and say *yes*...or refuse and say *no*...and move forward in God-confidence. But when the faith and peace of mind isn't there, this principle from Romans 14 regarding doubtful things comes to my rescue:

> *When in doubt, don't!*
> (or, put another way)
> *When in doubt, it's out!*

You Are Called to a Life of Wisdom

Prayer is how we seek the *will of God*—Remember, *No decision made without prayer!* And guess what? Prayer is also how we seek the *wisdom of God*.

> If any of you lacks wisdom, he should *ask God...and it will be given to him* (James 1:5).

Do you want to discover God's will in your life? Then you must not fail to ask Him for His wisdom. And how will we recognize it?

Wisdom fears the Lord—"The fear of the LORD is the beginning of wisdom" (Proverbs 9:10). That means being careful about life and about rushing ahead of God's will...and perhaps missing it altogether. That means there is a deep respect for God and a worshipful "fear" of Him. Therefore, don't try to impress or please others. Instead seek to live out one passion in your life—that of pleasing God, of finding favor with Him, of walking in His will.

So pray! Talk things over with the Lord *before* you act, *before* you make a move, and *before* you say a word! Learn to say, "Let me pray about that and get back to you."

Wisdom applies God's Word to everyday life—Do you ever wonder if a day is all that important? Yet, if you think about it, all you really have for doing God's will is a day—today! Jesus Himself told us not to postpone, wait, think, and wonder about tomorrow. He said, "Do not worry about tomorrow, for tomorrow will worry about itself. Each day has enough trouble of its own" (Matthew 6:34).

In other words, handling today with all of its demands, quirks, and surprises will require all of your effort, all of your strength, all of your focus on God's wisdom. You will be called upon to walk and act with wisdom and according to God's will all day long...around every corner and in every encounter.

> "Everything you do, every decision you make, every relationship you have, will be affected by your ability to apply wisdom to your experiences."[2]

So, how was your yesterday? And how is your today going? Be sure you pray yourself through your every day! Seek God's wisdom as the crises and curveballs of your day arrive as surely as the steady pounding of an ocean surf hits the shore.

Wisdom sees life from God's perspective—What is God's perspective? Here are a few observations from Proverbs.

> The fool envies the wealthy.
> The fool scorns his elders.
> The fool does not ask advice.
> The fool hates his neighbor.
> The fool sleeps his life away.
> The fool squanders his money.
> The fool despises wisdom.
> The fool speaks slander.
> The fool lies.
> The fool talks too much.
> The fool argues and quarrels.

And there's more! But the real question is, Are *you* seeing and living life from God's perspective? Beloved, *prayer* makes the difference! *Prayer* sets the wise woman apart from the "fools" just described. Taking time to close your eyes in prayer helps open them to God's way of seeing things.

And be prepared—*God* sees life from a completely different angle (Isaiah 55:8-9). That's why wisdom is such a distinctive mark. It dramatically separates you from the masses and makes all the difference in the choices and decisions you make.

Wisdom follows the best course of action—You know, it's really easy to *know* the right thing to do. In fact, the Bible says wisdom is calling out in the streets, on the corners, in all the public places (Proverbs 1:20-21). Wisdom is everywhere! It's available...and it's free! But the final indicator of wisdom is to *do* the right thing.

That's why we must *pray* for a heart of wisdom. On our own it's easy to be a fool...and almost impossible to walk in godly wisdom. That's why we need God's help. Unfortunately, Solomon, the wisest man in the world, possessed wisdom and *knew* the right things to do and could tell it to others. But he failed to continue to *do* what he knew...and became a fool. So we need to decide to access God's wisdom and put it to use in our lives. Praying over our decisions gives our hearts that extra boost when it comes to taking the best course of action.

My Checklist for Prayer

✓   *Commit to pray*—The surest way to miss God's will and God's best is to not pray—to not even pause and ask Him. And the surest way to be sure you discover God's will is, of course, to pray. So learn to say, "Let me pray about that and get back to you." Practice it in front of your mirror if you have to!

And now for some action! On the next page share what you did and when you did it. Make your own *No decision made*

> "Prayer is the first thing, the second thing, and the third thing necessary for a believer. Pray, then, my dear Christian, pray, pray, and pray."[3]

without prayer commitment. Write it out, put it in a special place, remember it, and rule your life by it. And don't forget to practice your motto for life: "Let me pray about that and get back to you." Keep track of how many times you say this when you are asked to do something this week, and write it here.

✓ *Set up to pray*—Purpose that from now on, *every* opportunity and *every* decision that must be made about *every*thing in your life will make its way onto your prayer page. Should you volunteer at work or school? Accept a date or go to a party? Get a part-time job? Attend college (and which college)? How should you spend your money...or your precious time and energy? Nothing is too small or too big to be prayed over. You are praying to know God's will for every detail of your life...and *that's* a big thing!

Make your own "Decisions to Make" prayer page. Then begin to fill it with the large or small decisions you must make. After all, it's *your* life! And that's important—vitally important!—not only to you, but to God!

Read again the prayer concerns above. What are yours? What decisions must you make? List both small and large issues that require your prayers now.

✓   *Pray faithfully*—Any and all decisions you must
     make are important. You can begin by using the
     scriptures shared on the page at the end of this
     chapter. The verses are like weapons for warfare. Be
     sure you pull them out of your arsenal and use them!
     Which one(s) do you like the best and why?

     The best way to begin to build an arsenal for deci-
     sion-making through prayer is to memorize three
     important verses. So write out each one on a card,
     carry them with you, and "write them on the tablet of
     your heart" (Proverbs 7:3)—memorize them! Which
     verse will you begin with? Write it here and let the
     memorizing and praying begin!

✎ Answering God's Call to You

As we leave this oh-so-brief overview of faith and wisdom, please acknowledge the role these two spiritual elements play in your decision-making process. They work mightily to help you find the will of God. I've referred to prayer many times in this book as being like a gem, a fantastic jewel with many flashing facets. And faith and wisdom are twin qualities in the glorious rock of prayer.

And, my dear praying friend, when you have answered God's call to prayer, when you have prayed, sought, and received God's faith, wisdom, and will, and when you have made your decision, praise Him! Praise God that you can ask Him through prayer for His faith and wisdom to guide your choices. Praise Him that you have done the praying, you have done the seeking, and you have made the best decision you can as you have sought His will.

Then proceed full-speed ahead with complete confidence that you are in the will of God. When yours is a seeking heart, He can guide and direct you as you go. Like a car that is tuned up and gassed up and turned on, He can steer you as you go. Then, all joy! Your life can bring Him the praise and honor and glory He so richly deserves!

Again, praise Him!

Putting God's Wisdom to Work in Your Life

What can you do about decision-making and the will of God? Follow this scriptural battle plan. These "weapons" work for every area of your life and lead you toward God's best.

First, ask God for help. Pray, "Lord, Your Word says in James 1:5, 'If any of you lacks wisdom, he should ask God...and it will be given to him.' So here I am, Lord! I need wisdom, and I'm asking You for it! Please reveal Your wisdom in this matter."

Next, pull James 4:17 out of your arsenal and pray, "And, Lord, Your Word says 'Anyone, then, who knows the good he ought to do and doesn't do it, sins.' Lord, I don't want to sin. I want to do the right thing, the good thing. So I've got to know what that is. Please show me the right thing so I can do it!"

Finally, reach for Proverbs 3:5 and 6 and pray, "And, Lord, Your Word says to 'trust in the LORD with all your heart and lean not on your own understanding; in all your ways acknowledge him, and he will make your paths straight.' I don't want to rely on my own heart, so I'm asking You right now, Lord, to guide my footsteps. What is the right thing to do here? What is the right decision? What is the path You want me to walk in? What is the *right way*?"

Six Scriptural Reasons to Pause and Pray

Revelation of God's will—"Trust in the LORD with all your heart and lean not on your own understanding; in all your ways acknowledge him, and he will make your paths straight" (Proverbs 3:5-6).

Clarity of God's will—"The way of the sluggard is blocked with thorns, but the path of the upright ['is made plain,' KJV]" (Proverbs 15:19).

Discernment of God's will—"All a man's ways seem innocent to him, but motives are weighed by the LORD" (Proverbs 16:2).

Insight into God's will—"All man's ways seem right to him, but the LORD weighs the heart" (Proverbs 21:2).

Blessing of God's will—"He who trusts in himself is a fool, but he who walks in wisdom is kept safe" (Proverbs 28:26).

Patience for God's will—"It is not good to have zeal without knowledge, nor to be hasty and miss the way" (Proverbs 19:2).

Would You Like to Know More?
Check It Out!

Read Romans 14:5 and 23 and 1 John 3:21. What difference should prayer and careful thought make in your choices and your confidence?

Read Acts 4:23-31. After praying, how did the early Christians act in faith and confidence?

Good decisions—God-based decisions!—require God's wisdom. What do these verses reveal about wisdom or what is wise?

Proverbs 9:10—

Matthew 6:33-34—

Proverbs 1:10-19—

Proverbs 1:20-23—

What do these verses say about *your* responsibility for walking in wisdom? List them here.

My List of Things I Don't Want to Forget...
...from This Chapter

When You Must Make a Decision...Pray for Understanding!

Yes, but...

Are these the two words you are thinking right about now? Are you wondering about God's will and how to find it? Are you feeling a bit uncertain about how everything adds up and fits together to indicate His will? Well, let's change your hesitation to three words—

Yes, but...how?

—and let me now share a few final *how's*. Let's look at the final step in the process I've been outlining for "Finding God's Will Through Prayer": *Pray for understanding*. When you pray for understanding, you will know more about God's will for you and the issues in your life.

Four Questions for Your Heart

It's hard to explain, but when we pray—when we do consult the Lord and wait upon Him for His direction—we *do* receive direction and confidence from God. Somehow He is able to impress His will upon our seeking hearts. And through Him we are able to understand what His will is.

So I have four questions that I ask my heart during prayer. I ask them in my effort to seek God's answers and guidance. While I'm praying about decisions that must be made, these four questions lead me right along the path of finding God's will. They help me to discover God's will for *me*, and they will work for you, too, as you seek His will for *you*. After all, God wants us to know His will. Why else would He ask or expect us to do it (Ephesians 6:6)? To begin your walk through these four questions, understand that honestly answering Questions 1 and 2 will surface your *motives*. Some of your motives will be pure and good, and others will be selfish and evil. After all, as Jeremiah pointed out, "The heart is deceitful above all things and beyond care. Who can understand it?" (Jeremiah 17:9)!

Then, as you continue on with your decision-making through prayer, you'll discover that Questions 3 and 4 will surface your *convictions*—what you know and believe the Word of God says about your decisions. Here's how this exercise has worked for me.

Question 1: Why would I do this?—One day I received a phone call from someone in my church asking me to teach a series of Bible classes. As I began praying, I asked *Why would I do this?* I could hardly believe that the first response that popped out of my heart was one of those sinful, wicked motives! My heart replied in answer to this question, *Oh, my name will be in the bulletin! Everyone will see my name in the bulletin as a great Bible teacher!*

I don't have to tell you that such a prideful response would *never* be a good reason to say *yes* to anything! No, the kinds of answers you and I are looking for as women after God's own heart include "because God would be glo-rified...because God's Word would be lifted up...because lives would be helped and changed...because the purpose of this Bible study is God-honoring."

You see the difference, right? In these heart-responses we are certainly getting closer to pure motives and solid rea-sons for saying *yes* than I was with the sickening response that my name would appear in the church bulletin!

So what did I do with such an answer? I wrote it down on the prayer page I created for this decision entitled "Teach Women's Bible Study." On the spot, I confessed to God how *wrong* such a thought/motive was! Then I drew a line through the answer and placed the page in the "Deci-sions to Make" section of my prayer notebook so I could look at it each day while I prayed about it...and record the progress being made toward making a decision—one hopefully based in God's wisdom!

And why did I write down such an awful answer on my prayer page? Because if it came out of my heart once, it would probably come out of it more than once! And I wanted a record of my conviction that teaching God's holy Word for such a *sinful* reason would be *wrong*. It would definitely *not* be God's will if based solely on such a reason.

Question 2: Why would I not do this?—Here's another instance, one when I was invited to speak at a v-e-r-y large women's event. On Day 1 of praying about this opportu-nity for ministry (labeled "Speak at Women's Event"), I first asked *Why would I do this?* and recorded my answers.

Then I asked *Why would I not do this?* And in rushed the answer, *Oh, I'm afraid! I've never done anything this large or in front of this many women before. I'm afraid!*

Well, both you and I know that fear is never a valid reason for refusing to do anything...if God is asking us to do it. Oh no! Our God has promised to supply *all* our needs (Philippians 4:19)—and that includes power in weakness and courage in the face of fear. Our God has promised that His grace will *always* be "sufficient" (2 Corinthians 12:9) when we need it to do His will. And "God did not [I repeat, *not!*] give us a spirit of timidity, but a spirit of power, of love and of self-discipline" (2 Timothy 1:7).

The "fear factor" is certainly one that should be acknowledged and dealt with and prayed about. But fear should never be a reason for saying *no*.

So I acknowledged it. I recorded my heart-response of fear...and then I drew a line through it. I can tell you that *every* day that I prayed over that invitation, my heart immediately muttered, "I'm afraid!" And *every* day I was able to look at that first answer with the line marked boldly through it and the scripture reference "2 Timothy 1:7!" written just as boldly next to it.

Now, what if my answer had been: *Ah, that'll be a lot of work...or take a lot of time...or I just don't feel like doing that?* Or, *I'd have to give up going to the mall...or sacrifice some time with my friends...to do that ministry?*

Well, you get the picture! Write it down, whatever your lame answer is, confess your laziness to the Lord, draw a line through it, and go on praying. You've just surfaced a weakness (maybe even a character flaw), one that you'll probably have to deal with again and again as you seek to *do* (note the energy that is required!) God's will, whatever doing it takes.

Now on to Questions 3 and 4, the ones that surface your *convictions,* what you know and believe to be right or wrong according to the Bible.

Question 3: Why should I do this?—When it was clear that my 93-year-old dad was dying from cancer, my Jim and I had a decision to make. We needed to know how much time I could—and should—give to help out and be present with him as he declined.

Practically, it was an easy decision for us. Our daughters were both married and the nest at home was empty. Also, I didn't have a job outside the home, so my time was my own to manage, and it was available so that I could help.

But most of all, the decision was made easier for us because both Jim and I believed this was one way we could follow the Bible's command to "honor your father and your mother" (Exodus 20:12 and Ephesians 6:2). As a couple we had a conviction about what the Bible said. Therefore, we believed I should do as much as I could to help.

My answers seemed to be lining up to something we could act on with confidence, with faith. Of course, we realized there would be a sacrifice of time, money (for airline tickets and long-distance phone calls), and companionship with one another. Yet we both believed helping my dad (who was 1,500 miles away) was the right thing to do. I had Jim's blessing, approval, and support. And my daughters certainly didn't need me at home.

So off I went to Oklahoma…on the six o'clock morning flight from Los Angeles to Tulsa every Monday morning, and back every Thursday evening when one of my brothers came to take over for the weekend. Little did we know when we prayed—and when God guided us into His will—that those commutes would go on for almost one entire year!

But, my dear young friend, *because* of the prayer process and *because* of praying to understand God's will in this decision, we were committed to do what it took and to see it through. And both Jim and I had perfect peace of mind and heart. To this day, we will tell you that we have no regrets. And here's another blessing! God's grace was sufficient for both of us during every minute of every day for that year.

> "The will of God will never lead you where the grace of God cannot keep you."[1]

And I need to say very clearly: *Your* answers to *your* prayer concerns and *your* "decisions to make" will probably turn out completely differently than it would for someone else. You and others will be at different stages in life. Your home life will be different than that of your peers. Your parents may have strong opinions and encourage you in a direction that differs from that of your best friends. You may have a part-time job or school responsibilities (choral group, pep squad, school newspaper, sports team) that make it impossible to do some things that "everyone else" is able to do.

So what can you do? *Pray!* Pray and pray and pray for an understanding of what God's perfect will is *for you!* As you pray, He *will* lead you to find it! And, blessing upon blessings, it will be tailor-made...*just for you!*

> Ask yourself, What would Jesus do, and what would Jesus have me do?

Question 4: Why should I not do this?—At one time I had an issue I prayed about long and hard. I agonized over trying to make some kind of decision. I turned to God's Word and read in the Book of Proverbs:

> The way of a fool seems right to him, but a wise man listens to advice (Proverbs 12:15).

> Listen to advice and accept instruction, and in the end you will be wise (Proverbs 19:20).

So I took the three pages of notes out of my prayer notebook where I had been recording my prayer progress each day on this particular item and gave them to my husband. As I handed them to Jim, I explained, "I just can't get any direction on this prayer request. Can you see if there is anything I'm missing?"

Well, dear Jim read through the decision that needed to be made then looked at my thoughts that I had written down. He knew I'd been praying about the situation. He went over the pros and cons, and then he gave me his advice. Since I respect Jim's opinion and I know he honors God, I accepted his take on the situation. And I made my decision!

And what about you? You don't have a husband you can turn to right now, but you do have mentors, teachers, and parents. So be a "wise" woman! Seek advice from people you trust and admire. And may I encourage you to especially pass your decisions by your mom and dad for their blessing and approval? They love you and will help you. I know it can be hard to consult your parents, but if you desire *God's* direction and blessing, *He* says to "obey your parents" and to "honor" them "that it may go well with you" (Ephesians 6:1-3). *Their* input will help guide you to *God's* will.

As I said, these are examples of how this four-question exercise has worked for me. And now I'm praying it will help *you* to better understand the will of God for *your* life...and your every decision. You will want to use these four questions for each and every decision you pray about, large or small.

Ask these questions about *every* prayer concern. Should you sign up for a Bible study? Volunteer for a ministry? Attend the Saturday youth conference at church? Apply to a certain college. Accept a date? Continue to go out with a certain guy? Purchase that DVD? Go to that concert? Sign up for an after-school sport or extracurricular activity? Go out with your friends the night of your little brother or sister's birthday party?

On and on goes the list of issues and concerns that make up a woman's wonderful—and challenging!—life. And for every single one of them, you will definitely come closer to discovering God's will by first determining *No decision made without prayer!* and then by asking these four questions as you pray for understanding.

My Checklist for Prayer

✓   *Do it now!*—Stop making decisions you don't pray about! So far we've learned that a life of *faith*, a life of *wisdom*, and a life of *understanding* are all realized when we pray. So do it now! Make the decision that affirms *No decision made without prayer.* Begin putting every activity and possibility on trial through prayer.

Yes, *every* activity! There are plenty of activities that will compete for your time, attention, and energy. But which one or ones should you accept or attempt to accomplish? Put each one on trial. Pray over them. Ask God for His wisdom to choose your activities carefully and intelligently. And ask your parents or pastor, too. What glorious confidence you'll have in your heart as you walk—in God's will—into an activity or commitment *knowing* that it was chosen through and after much prayer!

Wow! Talk about becoming the woman after God's own heart that you've dreamed of becoming! Oh, dear one, prayer is the key! Prayer is the answer! Prayer is the way! When you answer God's call to pray, you become the woman He designed *you* to be—one who walks with Him in faith, wisdom, and understanding; one who walks confidently and graciously in His will.

Can you remember a decision you made without any help or guidance from God or others? Jot it down below. What happened? What would you do differently now, and why? Also name two or three people you will consult the next time you have to make an important decision.

✓ *Do it now!*—If you haven't already done it, create a "Decisions to Make" section in your prayer notebook or journal...*now!* (If you haven't yet created or purchased a notebook or journal, do it now, too.) Instead of reaping "the trouble in life" that quickly saying *yes* brings your way, *pray!*

> "One-half the trouble in life can be traced to saying *yes* too quickly."[2]

And speaking of saying *yes* or *no,* what decision did the young man Daniel and his friends have to make in Daniel 1:1-20? What impresses you most about these bold guys many scholars believe were teenagers?

✓ *Do it now!*—If you haven't already, make a list of the current decisions you need to make. (I counted 14 on my list just this morning.) Create a page for each one and place them in your "Decisions to Make" section. Then prayerfully make your way through them.

And here's a quick fix along the way...just in case you are pressured for a quick answer, *Say no!* And say *no* often. In your life, as in art, less is more. You have prayed long and hard to know God's will. And finally, at last, it is evident what His will is. So, as you step into His good and perfect will, be prepared. You will now need to pray for God's help to say *no*...to yourself when you weaken or get tired, to your flesh when you want something other than God's will, to last-minute invitations to do something else, to the excuses you come up with as to why you don't think you can follow God's will.

Pray to God to help you make it through just this one day of walking in *His* plan and *His* will! And tomorrow plan to do the same. Realize, too, that if and when you are high-pressured into making a hurried decision, "the best answer is always *no*, because *no* is more easily changed to *yes* than *yes* is to *no*."[3]

Look again at Daniel and his friends, you know, the guys who said *no* to the king? What happened in Daniel 3:13-18? Again, what impresses you most about these men after God's own heart?

✎ Answering God's Call to You

Please pardon all of my exclamation marks and the *Do it now's*. But, beloved, this is getting most urgent! For two chapters we have addressed the importance of finding God's will. We admit we desire the benefits that walking in God's will reaps in life. But it is now definitely time to *do* something! It is time to move out in action. To make your commitment. To build your notebook or purchase a journal. To begin sweetly saying, "I'll have to pray about that. Let me get back to you"…instead of blurting out (like I did), "Sure I'll do it" or "No how! No way! No ma'am!"

Again, remember that God expects us to do His will. He also gives us everything we need to do it—

—His all-sufficient grace (2 Corinthians 12:9),

—His "I can do everything through [Christ]" strength (Philippians 4:13),

—His supply of "all your need" (Philippians 4:19), and

—His promise of "everything we need for life and godliness" (2 Peter 1:3).

Finally, when making decisions, pray…and do a heart check. The condition of your *heart* and your *heart's desire* is vital to understanding and doing God's will. Why? Because God gives this final key to understanding and doing His will—you are to be "doing the will of God *from your heart*" (Ephesians 6:6)!

Now, how's your heart?

Would You Like to Know More? Check It Out!

Read Proverbs 3:5-6, looking at each word. What is God's promise regarding His will in verse 6?

What is your part in discovering God's will according to

verse 5a—

verse 5b—

verse 6—

As you think about your part in discovering God's will, on which point(s) do you tend to fail? How do you think prayer will help?

Write down one decision you are trying or needing to make. Create a prayer page for it, and begin praying through the four questions below. (Make notes here if you'd like.) If you make a decision on it this week, note how you made your decision or why you made it.

Question 1: Why would I do this?
(Remember to confess any unbiblical motives.)

Question 2: Why would I not do this?
(Remember to rule out anything that goes against God's Word.)

Question 3: Why should I do this?
(Remember to look for reasons from God's Word.)

Question 4: Why should I not do this?
(Remember your goal is to obey and please God.)

My List of Things I Don't Want to Forget...
...from This Chapter

Discovering God's Formula for Effective Prayer

The Time—and Times—
of Prayer

As a child growing up in a home where both parents were schoolteachers, great emphasis was put on learning. Not only were my three brothers and I to learn everything we could, but my parents continued expanding their knowledge. Even during the summer when school was out, one of my parents would go away for a few weeks to complete graduate-level courses toward yet another advanced educational degree.

Well, not for me! I determined. I foolishly thought when I graduated from high school, *No more school for me! I'm out of here!* But now I know better. I now know what you know and what my parents knew—all of life is about learning.

You and I are constantly learning how to do a variety of things, aren't we? We spend hours learning to use a computer, fix our hair, play the piano, or play a sport. On and on our learning opportunities go! And prayer is no different. Read what one man says about learning to pray...and the time it takes to do so:

> It is sheer nonsense for us to imagine that we can learn the high art of getting guidance through communion with the Lord without being willing to set aside time for it and learn to pray.[1]

So far in this book we've looked at God's Word and discovered some things about prayer, the meaning of prayer, and the blessings of prayer. But be prepared! Our focus is switching here. We're going to now learn more about the in's and out's of prayer, about "God's Formula for Effective Prayer"—a formula we can easily follow.

And we are pressing toward the finish line, toward the end of our book. So hang on tight! And hang in there! There will be a new flavor to these fun chapters. They are filled with motivating stories and practical tips to inspire your heart to pray. I like to think of this section as the "sparkle" that the facets in the gem of prayer produce.

The first component of God's formula is...

A Time for Personal Prayer

Do you ever wonder when to pray? If there is a good, better, or best time to pray? Well, looking at some of God's people at prayer shows us a few answers.

 Abraham prayed early at daybreak.

 Jacob wrestled in prayer all night long.

 Samuel, too, prayed all night.

The psalmist advised that we pray evening, morning, at noon, day and night, at midnight, with the dawning of the morning, and in the night watches.

 Other saints prayed three times a day, even up to seven times a day!

 Jesus prayed in the morning, prayed through the night, prayed before eating, and prayed at midnight in the Garden of Gethsemane.

 Finally, we are to pray always (Ephesians 6:18) and without ceasing (1 Thessalonians 5:17).

It's easy to see that a common denominator for these faithful pray-ers was a definite time, or times, of prayer.

A Time for Emergency Prayer

In addition to a set time of prayer, "God's Formula for Effective Prayer" includes calling out to Him in a time of emergency. In fact, God pleads with us to "call to me." These words come from Jeremiah 33:3. The full instruction to God's prophet was, "Call to me and I will answer you and tell you great and unsearchable things you do not know." Many people refer to this verse as "God's phone number—JER333." And there are definitely those horrifying *times* of emergency or crisis when we will need to call God's number!

It is during these crisis times that we must do what I once heard described as 9-1-1 praying. Do you realize all that goes on when a 9-1-1 call is made? When you (or even a toddler!) dial those three numbers, you are almost instantly connected with the emergency dispatcher. And in front of that dispatcher is a readout that lists the telephone number you are calling from and the name of the person it is listed to, complete with an address. Also ready to respond are the paramedics and the police and fire departments.

Callers to the 9-1-1 line may not even know what's going on. They're just calling in a time of great need. They may not know what the problem is, or they may not be able to say what the problem is. They may not know where they are. They may be out of control and hysterical because something has happened to a loved one...or to them...or has been witnessed by them.

But the truth is, the dispatcher doesn't actually need the caller to say anything. All a person has to do is make the call...and help is on the way!

Reaching Out to God in Prayer

So it is with the times in our life when we are desperate and in pain. All we have to do is reach out to God in a 9-1-1 call. Just like God said to Jeremiah, "Call to me and *I will answer you*."

Sure, sometimes we're hysterical. Sometimes we just don't know how to handle what is happening. Sometimes there aren't words to say about what is happening, or there isn't the energy to say anything. But God hears. He knows our trouble. And help is already on the way! He has already begun to bring the

"To flee unto God is the only stay which can support us in our afflictions." —John Calvin

answer, the solution, the help, the grace needed when we call upon Him.

And this is what Hannah did when she had no child... and only God could help. Nehemiah called out to God when the city of Jerusalem, God's city, was lying in ruin and only God could change that. The church prayed a 9-1-1 prayer for Peter when he awaited death in prison. And Hezekiah cried out to the Lord when he encountered an illness unto death. Paul beseeched God over and over regarding his thorn in the flesh, something that would not go away, something that caused him great trouble. Moses raised his prayers in the midst of battle. And our Savior poured out His heart to His Father when preparing to meet death on a cross.

In these types and times of trouble—and emergency!—we must call out to the Lord in prayer.

Hearing God's Call to Prayer

"Call to me," saith the Lord. This is a clear command from the God of the universe to our hearts to call *to* and to call *on* Him! His desire for us to call out and pray to Him cannot be missed—"Call to me and I will answer you and tell you great and unsearchable things you do not know" (Jeremiah 33:3). Did you notice that in this call to prayer, you only have to do *one thing*—call upon God? Then He does *two things* for you—He promises to answer you *and* to tell you great and unsearchable things!

So turn your heart upward! In your distress and your concern for others, reach out to God in prayer. Call out to Him, the One who possesses all of the power that exists...as well as all of the comfort, mercy, and lovingkindness. Freely shoot your prayers heavenward. As many as you like! As many as you can! And as many as it takes!

And then stand back, faithful pray-er. For the God of the universe *will* answer you. And, as if that weren't enough, He will also *tell* you wonderful—incredible!—things you do not know.

Talking to God About Your Life

It's obvious, isn't it, that to answer God's call to prayer we must develop our own time for prayer? To make time to talk the important things in our life over with God, we must nail down a time that's best for us. And the exciting thing is, it can be *any* time! But it should also be a *set* time, a certain time, a specific time. That's the way it is with special appointments. For instance, there was a time when I chose early morning as my set time. At that time in my life, if I didn't pray early…I didn't pray! Then things changed (as they always do!), and I switched my time, choosing to pray first thing after everyone left the house in the morning.

So pick *your* time—the one that fits *your* lifestyle best—and then follow the three steps in the "My Checklist for Prayer." You'll be well on your way to becoming a woman of prayer!

My Checklist for Prayer

✓   *First, get organized*—Set a time for prayer. Plan it, schedule it, protect it, and keep it as if it were an appointment.

Perhaps you remember dating a special guy and how wonderful that was? Can you recall how you relished the thought of every time you were going to be able to see him? You had a "date"...and a date on the calendar! Why, you were so excited that you put in extra time in preparation to get yourself ready to meet him, taking great care to be at your best.

Well, the same should be true concerning you and a regular date with God to pray. This message came home loud and clear to me during one of my husband's annual two-week training camps for the Army Reserve. Something came up that meant I had to call him at exactly 5:45 A.M. So the night before, I set my alarm for 3:30 A.M. (!!!) to allow for the two-hour difference between our time zones...and some time to splash cold water on my face and drink a cup of coffee.

The night before I also wrote out a list of the questions I needed to ask Jim, knowing there wouldn't be much time to talk with him. I even laid out a pen and paper for writing down Jim's answers and advice.

The next day when the alarm went off, I tore out of bed, went through my waking-up drill, and sat...watching the clock, watching the clock, watching the clock. Finally, at last! at 3:44 (my time) I dialed the special phone number...and Jim picked up the phone and said, "Hello, Elizabeth."

Now, while I was sitting there with my heart racing in anticipation, sitting there waiting and going through all my preparations, I was also sitting there thinking, *Why can't I do this every morning to talk with God? Why can't I prepare to meet with the Lord in prayer the night before—get out a pad and pen, be organized about what I want to say to Him and need to ask of Him? Why can't I set the alarm, get right up and splash cold water on my face, have a cup of coffee or a glass of juice, sit and wait for that appointment with God, meet with Him right on schedule, and hear Him say (so to speak), "Hello, Elizabeth!"? Why can't I take the time and care to share my concerns with God in prayer and write down the answers He gives me?*

And the answer was crystal clear! I needed to *set* a time for prayer...so that I could *have* a time for prayer.

And the same is true for you. Get organized. What time is best for you? Pick a time and write your daily "date" with God right on your daily calendar. In fact, why don't you figure out when you can pray every day this week. Write it down here and follow through. I know you can do it, and you'll be amazed at the results!

✓ *Second, get ready*—Begin the night before and the morning of. It's true that...

> — the prepared person succeeds and the unprepared one fails;

> — 75 percent of victory and achievement is traced back to preparation—maybe even 80 percent!

Prepare by *thinking about your prayer time*... about how much you look forward to it, about how important prayer is to your spiritual growth, about how crucial it is that your loved ones be prayed for, about the sheer joy of being obedient in this commanded spiritual discipline, about the unbelievable privilege you have to commune with and worship God in this most intimate way.

Then continue your preparations by *thinking about your needs* during your prayer time. My needs for contacting my husband included a quarter-hour head-start (for clearing my head!), some nourishment, a pad and pen—all of which I also need for my daily prayer time.

Do your prayer needs include setting out your favorite pen and a prayer notebook or journal and making a cup of hot choco-late? What else? (Please answer on the next page.) I even read about one woman who feels like she needs to brush her teeth before she "talks" to God.

> "Before beginning, prepare carefully."
> —Cicero

Know what you need to do for making the most of your time of prayer.

Finally, prepare the night before by *getting to bed on time*. Schedule backward from your ideal prayer time to allow yourself the sleep time you need. Be ruthless as you beeline to bed. And don't forget to set the alarm! Then pray...to get up to pray!

Scheduling is everything when it comes to doing what you want to do. So what do you need to do in advance to get up and pray tomorrow morning? What time did you choose for prayer? And what time will you need to get to bed?

✓ *Third, get up*—And how is this accomplished? By getting up! I won't belabor the point, but I know people who sleep with their cell phones *and* telephones next to the bed. And believe me (and you know it, too), whenever either phone rings, they jump to answer! Their hearts are pounding, the adrenaline is flowing, and the blood is pumping...and they're up! (And it's just a telephone!)

"Mind over mattress!"

This must become your response to your alarm's sound. Treat it like it is God calling you to prayer. It's your Commander-in-Chief. It's the Ruler of your life. It's the Master bidding you to join Him in prayer. So...get up!

Now, review the list of "times" for prayer in this chapter under the subhead "A Time for Personal Prayer." How can you follow in the steps of these people who prayed? Again, what time have you chosen to be "your" time to answer God's call to prayer?

✎ Answering God's Call to You

My dear friend, although prayer is a sacred privilege, in some ways it is no different than any other activity you choose to undertake—you must first want to learn about prayer so you can enjoy praying. Won't you answer God's call to prayer by the simple act of choosing a time for prayer? Then be faithful. Keep your commitment. Show up at the appointed time...and revel in the joy of communing with Him.

> "He who has learned to pray has learned the greatest secret of a holy and a happy life."[2]

The Difference Prayer Makes

I got up early one morning
And rushed right into the day;
I had so much to accomplish
That I didn't take time to pray.

Problems just tumbled about me,
And heavier came each task;
"Why doesn't God help me?" I wondered.
He answered: "You didn't ask."

I wanted to see joy and beauty—
But the day toiled on, gray and bleak;
I wondered why God didn't show me,
He said, "But you didn't seek."

I tried to come into God's presence,
I used all my keys at the lock;
God gently and lovingly chided:
"My child, you didn't knock."

I woke up early this morning
And paused before entering the day;
I had so much to accomplish
That I had to take time to pray.[3]

Would You Like to Know More?
Check It Out!

What do you learn about the time and times of prayer from these people?

Abraham in Genesis 19:27—

Nehemiah in Nehemiah 2:1-5—

David in Psalm 5:3—

Peter in Matthew 14:25-33—

Jesus in Mark 1:35—

Can you think of others? Who are they, and when did they pray?

Can you think of changes you need to make in your prayer-life?

Read Mark 14:32-42. What was Jesus' distressing situation here?

What words describe His agony?

How did He handle it?

What did He ask of Peter, James, and John?

How long was Jesus' time of prayer?

How many of these times of prayer did Jesus have?

What is your most distressing issue at this time, and what does Jesus' example teach you to do...or to do better?

Who do you know who is currently in a time of distress? How can you pray faithfully for him or her?

My List of Things I Don't Want to Forget...
...from This Chapter

9

The Place and Posture of Prayer

I'm sure you've met people who impacted your life, making your time with them especially meaningful. Well, that's what happened to me one wonderful weekend in the beautiful state of Washington.

After a women's event, I stayed overnight in the home of the retreat coordinator so I could catch the first flight home the next morning. As Jennifer and I sat in her kitchen (where else!), she told me how she and her husband had purchased their home from her mother after her dad died and her mom moved to a smaller place.

Then Jennifer shared, "Elizabeth, we remodeled the whole house. But there was one thing in the house that I couldn't touch, and that's this kitchen counter." She went on to explain, "All my life, every morning when I came down from sleep, the first thing I saw was my mother, sitting right here at the end of this counter, praying. That's why I couldn't touch this counter. It was my mother's prayer place."

But the story goes on. The next morning when I came down the stairs that entered the kitchen, there was my hostess, sitting on a stool at the end of that kitchen counter with her Bible and notebook spread out, having her prayer time. You guessed it—Jennifer had made it her prayer place, too!

Is There a Proper Place to Pray?

We already know that we can pray to God at any time, day or night. God never sleeps, and He is always available to His people (Psalm 121:3). His ears are always open to us, and He hears our prayers (1 Peter 3:12). But let's take our desire to answer God's call to prayer and to discover His formula for effective prayer one step further and ask, *Is there a correct or proper place to pray?*

A quick look at both Old Testament and New Testament pray-ers shows us that we can approach God anywhere with our prayers. For example,

— King David prayed in a cave (Psalm 57).

— The Israelites prayed in the wilderness (1 Kings 8:33-34,47-49).

— Elijah prayed in an upper room in a house (1 Kings 17:20).

— Daniel prayed in his room (Daniel 2:19).

— Sailors prayed in their ship (Jonah 1:13-14).

— Peter prayed on a housetop (Acts 10:9).

— Lydia and a group of women prayed by the river side (Acts 16:13).

— Paul and Silas prayed in stocks in a prison (Acts 16:25).

— Paul and the disciples at Tyre prayed on the beach (Acts 21:5).

God's people are to pray *every*where (1 Timothy 2:8)... from *any* place...at *any* time. We can pray while we're doing homework, while we're in the shower, while we're driving a car or riding in an airplane, while we're down on our knees working on a project, or while we're at the kitchen counter...like my friend did.

A Journey to a Place of Prayer

I was just thinking through my own journey into prayer and the variety of my places of prayer. My first prayer place was a table with a nice big area for all my prayer "things." For years I did my praying there. Then, for some reason, I switched my place of prayer to the sofa. I covered the couch, the floor, the coffee table—every square inch!—with all my prayer stuff and prayed to my heart's content.

After we moved, my next place of prayer was my bed. I l-o-v-e my bed! And there was plenty of room on it for my Bible, prayer notebook, colored markers, and, of course, every girl's favorite—the Kleenex box! That was my favorite place to pray...then. But as time went on, I moved down to the cuddly chair in my little office. There I had a floor-to-ceiling bookcase where every kind of tool (such as Bible commentaries) I would ever need during prayer was available (that is...until an earthquake demolished my office!).

But I have to report that no matter where I settled in to pray, my notebook has been my Number One mainstay and prayer tool for the 25-plus years I've been on my personal prayer journey. I keep all sorts of prayer "lists" in it. For instance…

I have a page for my own "Personal list"—my dreams of serving God and my goals for life. Then I have a "Family list" and a "People list." We've already discussed the necessity of a "Decisions-to-Make list." I also keep a "Spiritual Growth list" that's filled with resolutions and the lists of "alwayses" and "nevers" that you and I both hope and pray will become true in our conduct! All the projects I'm working on are on my "Projects list," and ministry events are on my "Ministry list." I even have a "Crisis list" for all the crises that are going on in my or my extended family and friends' lives at any given time!

Your prayer place will be different than mine. And the tools you use to make your prayer-life more powerful and efficient—and exciting!—will differ from mine. But, oh, what a thrill it will be to see your prayer place and your prayer plan—and your prayer-life!—evolve into something that is organized. That indicates a serious pray-er, a woman who is making her desire to pray a reality.

The Places of Prayer for Others

Would you like to know how some others have prayed and where their places of prayer were? Let's peek in on a few!

Susannah Wesley, the mother of the famous brothers, John and Charles Wesley, would simply pull her apron up over her head, and that provided an instant place of prayer for her. Maybe as the mother of ten children that's the only place she could find to pray! Those children, though, came to recognize their mother's apron as a "Do Not Disturb— Woman at Prayer" sign! (What's your sign?)

John Wesley, the son of Susannah and the founder of Methodism, had a "prayer chamber" in his home. Jim and I actually got to tour Wesley's home and stood for some time in his private prayer chamber. It has been preserved exactly as it was when this great man of God knelt there before the Almighty. It's a little room off his bedroom. And there's nothing in it except a table with a candlestick and a Greek New Testament on it and a small stool—sort of a kneeling stool.

The guide told us that this little room, this "prayer room," was "the powerhouse of Methodism." It was Mr. Wesley's prayer place. (Do you have a place or a room or, more importantly, a habit of praying that others could point to as "the powerhouse" of your life?)

John Fletcher, eighteenth-century theologian, was said to have stained the walls of his chamber with the breath of his prayers lifted from his prayer place. (How do the walls of your prayer place measure up?)

Early African converts to Christianity were very earnest and regular in their personal devotions. Each man would go out through the bush to a private place to pray. Soon the routine of trekking through the grass marked out distinct paths as the grass became beaten down. One look and everyone could tell if someone was faithful in prayer because his path was obvious. But if anyone began to neglect his prayer time, it was also quite obvious. And, sure enough, soon one of the brothers-in-Christ would come and say, "Brother, the grass grows on your path." (How's the "path" to your prayer place? Is it well used?)

Ruth Graham, the late wife of Billy Graham, believed we should leave our Bibles out and open someplace in our room or house so that "whenever there is a lull in the storms of life, we can grab a cup of coffee and sit down for a time of pure refreshment and companionship."[1] (So... where can you squeeze in a soda and enjoy some rich companionship with "the God of peace"?)

The Place of Prayer for You

Do any of these examples inspire you to find a special place to pray? Jesus said, "Go into your room, close the door and pray to your Father, who is unseen" (Matthew 6:6). Some would call such a room their "prayer closet," a place where their prayer-life is nurtured. One writer—and pray-er—points out,

> Oh! You can pray anywhere...but you are not likely to unless you are off in some quiet place shut in with God....Enter into thine inner chamber, and shut thy door. That door is important. It shuts out, and it shuts in....God is here in this shut-in spot. One must get alone to find out that he is never alone.[2]

Do whatever it takes to have *your* place of prayer. Whether it's a literal closet or some other place, create *your* secret place where you meet with the Lord to pray.

Is There a Proper Posture for Prayer?

Many Christians believe that kneeling is the biblical posture for prayer. We think immediately of Jesus kneeling in the Garden of Gethsemane to pray (Luke 22:41). Or of the apostle Paul kneeling on the beach with the elders from Ephesus and with his disciples in Tyre (Acts 20:36; 21:5).

It's true that many of God's people throughout time have prayed on their knees. For instance, in the early days of our republic a stranger asked at Congress how he would distinguish George Washington from the rest of the people. He was told that he could easily recognize him. When Congress goes to prayer, Washington is the gentleman who always kneels.

Also it was said of hymn-writer Fanny Crosby that she never attempted to write music or lyrics without first kneeling to pray about the undertaking. That meant she spent a great deal of time on her knees because she wrote more than 8,000 hymns of faith!

Then there is James, the leader of the church in Jerusalem. He was known as "camel knees" by the early church. "When they came to coffin him, it was like coffining the knees of a camel rather than the knees of a man, so hard, so worn, so stiff were they from prayer, and so unlike any other dead man's knees they had ever coffined."[3] (How are *your* knees, dear pray-er?)

I have also saved these few lines from a poem that points to the usefulness of praying on your knees.

Traveling on My Knees

Last night I took a journey
to a land across the sea.
I did not go by boat or plane,
I traveled on my knees.[4]

Praying on your knees is a graphic picture of one who is humble of heart. But, as biblical as kneeling may be, the Bible shows us a variety of postures for prayer.

❀ The people of God *bowed their heads* in worship (Exodus 4:31).

❀ Moses and Aaron repeatedly *fell on their faces* to pray (Numbers 16:22 is one instance).

❀ Hannah *stood* at the doorway of the tabernacle, praying (1 Samuel 1:12-14).

❀ David *sat* before the Lord and prayed (2 Samuel 7:18).

❀ David also *fasted* and *lay on the ground* all night praying (2 Samuel 12:16).

❀ Solomon *knelt* with his *hands spread out* toward heaven and prayed (1 Kings 8:54).

❀ Elijah *bowed down* and *put his face between his knees* and prayed (1 Kings 18:42; James 5:18).

❀ Jonah prayed to the Lord *from the stomach of a fish* (Jonah 2:1). (We can only imagine what his posture was during his impassioned prayer on that wild ocean voyage!)

❀ Ezra *bowed down*, wept, and prayed (Ezra 10:1).

❀ The tax collector *hung his head* and *beat on his breast*, and in humility of heart *stood* afar off and prayed (Luke 18:13).

❀ Jesus poured out His prayers *on His face* in the Garden of Gethsemane (Matthew 26:39).

The Bible does not give any final instruction on the "right" posture of our praying. But one thing is certain from these examples—These people's postures during prayer indicated what was going on in their hearts! Some were worshiping as God's law prescribed. Some were torn in emotional agony. Some were suffering personally, and some were suffering for others. Some were sorry over sin. Some were in battle, either literal war or for the lives and souls of others. Some were asking for a miracle. Some were joyful or thankful. Whatever emotion their life situation evoked, it was expressed in the posture of the pray-ers.

"When You Pray…"

Jesus cautions us not to use prayer as a means of getting attention. Our voice and posture of prayer can actually distract others and interfere with *their* prayer and worship. Prayer can also so easily be done for the wrong reasons. So be sure and check your motives for the manner in which you pray. Jesus advises us...

> when you pray, do not be like the hypocrites, for they love to pray standing in the synagogues and on the street corners, to be *seen by men* (Matthew 6:5).

Jesus continues His instruction on prayer by giving a solution for making sure we don't use prayer as an avenue for "showing off":

> But when you pray, go into your room, close the door and pray to your Father, who is unseen. Then your Father, who sees what is done in secret, will reward you (verse 6).

Notice in both verses the issue is not "if" you pray, but "when you pray." Jesus assumes that you (and I!) are going to pray. His people are called to pray, commanded to pray, expected to pray, and instructed on how to pray. But the issue is always the heart—whether or not your heart is right before God.

And, dear one, if your only desire is to worship God and praise Him and petition Him and pour out your heart to Him, then there will never be a wrong posture for your prayers. Why, you could even pray standing on your head, as the following discussion illustrates!

The Prayer of Cyrus Brown

"The proper way for man to pray,"
said Deacon Lemuel Keyes,
"the only proper attitude
is down upon his knees."

"Nay, I should say, the way to pray,"
said Reverend Dr. Wise,
"is standing straight with outstretched arms,
with rapt and upturned eyes."

"Oh, no, no no!"
said Elder Snow.
"Such posture is too proud.
A man should pray with eyes fast closed
and head contritely bowed."

"It seems to me his hands should be
austerely clasped in front,
with both thumbs pointing to the ground,"
said Reverend Dr. Blunt.

"Last year I fell in Hodgkins' well,
head first," said Cyril Brown,
"with both my heels a stickin' up,
my head a pointin' down.

"And I done prayed right then and there,
the best prayer I ever said,
the prayin'est prayer I ever prayed,
a standin' on my head!"[5]

My Checklist for Prayer

✓   *Describe*...your place of prayer—Do you have one? Share about it below. If you are having trouble praying with all of the distractions of a bustling family, with a phone that won't stop ringing, maybe a prayer closet is what you need.

Or are you homeless when it comes to prayer? Or a vagabond...you pray here a little, there a little, everywhere a little-little? Answer honestly. If either is true, then...

✓   *Decide*...where your place will be—Experiment. Move around. Sooner or later you'll feel "at home" and enjoy success in your prayer efforts. Your heart will tell you when you're "home"!

So describe away! Also take time to list any "prayer-home improvements" you can make.

✓ *Dedicate*...yourself to private prayer—It's fun and exciting to pray with others, to pray for one another, and to praise God together. Such times of group prayer are a thrilling part of "body life"—*koinonia*—among Christians. But be sure you spend the majority of your time in prayer *out* of the public eye... "praying in secret." Why?

First, it will affirm your motives for prayer. You can commune earnestly and sincerely and passionately with God with no distractions. It's just you and Him behind that closed door. So pray, dear one, to your "audience of One"!

And second, a "secret" prayer life allows you to focus on the real and personal—and private!—issues of life that you need to talk over with God. When you're alone you can concentrate your full energy and efforts for a more meaningful and productive time of prayer.

Just for this next week, keep a record of the amount of time you spend praying in private. What does your record-keeping reveal?

Monday _____   Friday _____

Tuesday _____   Saturday _____

Wednesday_____   Sunday _____

Thursday _____

✎ Answering God's Call to You

Dear friend, God is calling you to a life of prayer. Prayer is one act of worship and service that you can do at any time and in any place. So lift your voice to God. Yes, prayer is a blessing—but praying is not easy! Your life, like mine, is filled with a multitude of activities that can crowd out your times for prayer. And there is also the battle against your flesh as you struggle with sin and spiritual laziness. And since prayer is a spiritual exercise, if you aren't careful you can find yourself fleeing from the presence of the Lord because of a divided, impure, and empty heart.

My dear sister-in-prayer, I hope you'll join me so that we may answer God's call to prayer together. Let us lift our voices to His throne of grace!

Would You Like to Know More? Check It Out!

Read Matthew 6:5-6.

What are Jesus' instructions regarding a place of prayer?

What is Jesus' message regarding your motives in your prayer times?

What does Jesus teach regarding your heavenly Father?

After reflecting on these teachings, how important would you say it is to pray in private?

Review the list of people in the section in your book entitled "Is There a Proper Posture for Prayer?" What is the key message to your heart from these faithful pray-ers?

Read John 4:19-24. What is the most important element of true worship, of which prayer is a part?

My List of Things I Don't Want to Forget...
...from This Chapter

Developing
the Habit
of
Prayer

How Can I Learn to Pray?

When we began our pilgrimage into prayer, you and I set our sights—and our hearts—on answering God's call to prayer. The deep desire of our hearts was to make prayer a reality in our lives. And to launch our journey together, we took a look in the mirror and asked, "What keeps me from praying?" And now we have come full circle. We've considered some reasons we don't pray more often...and hopefully done something about them. We've also looked at some of the distressing circumstances in life that move us to pray...and learned that we must talk them over with God, pray for wisdom, and leave our requests with Him.

And now that we are turning our hearts toward the end of our wonderful journey together, it's time to ask and answer the question, How can I learn to pray? Let's discover how to put our efforts at prayer into warp speed. Here we go!

1. *Use a prayer list or notebook*—How many times have you been guilty of telling people you would pray for them—and then not doing it? When you heard their request or their

problem, you were deeply moved and genuinely desired to pray for them...but then you forgot all about it!

With a place to write down your prayer concerns, you improve your prayer-life immediately. Learn to carry a small spiral pad with you or a 3" x 5" card. Then, whenever people ask you to pray for them or share that they are struggling with an issue, write it down. Later on, move it to your prayer notebook and, of course, pray faithfully!

(And P.S. If it's at all possible, pray with hurting people on the spot. Your instant, on-the-spot prayer can give them immediate relief and peace in their hurting hearts.)

And how about your own life—your own problems and concerns? A prayer list or notebook, although physically only paper and cardboard, is a marvelous spiritual aid to your prayer-life. It's a tool that...

- ❀ orders your prayers,

- ❀ helps you remember who and what to pray for,

- ❀ serves as a visual reminder of God's faithfulness and goodness as He answers your prayer requests, and

- ❀ creates a historical accounting of God's workings in your life and in other people.

2. *Schedule a prayer time each day*—When you or I don't schedule something, it usually doesn't get done. And the same is true with prayer. You can think about praying. You can talk about praying. You can worry about praying. You can wish to be praying. You can even pray to be

praying! But until you schedule the act of prayer, it probably won't happen regularly.

So pick an amount of time and a set time. I began my personal journey into prayer with five minutes a day! My overriding principle was *Something is better than nothing!* My five minutes became the bait that drew me into experiencing sweet, precious times of prayer—many of those times extending on and on. Forget the clock! Once I was started, I couldn't stop! Sure, there were those days when five minutes was all there was. But I began small...and, in time, witnessed mighty effects! And the same will be true for you when you schedule a prayer time each day.

3. *Spend time praying with others*—The habit of praying is born and nurtured in private. But praying with others matures and enhances your prayer-life. Do you know some sisters-in-Christ who share your heart for prayer? Maybe you can establish a prayer group with those young women who share your passion. You can meet at the church, in homes, at school, or even in a park! Just be sure you actually pray when you get together. Answer God's call to prayer together.

4. *Pray using Scripture*—God not only loves to hear His own Word, but there is power in His Word. Indeed, "the word of God is living and active. Sharper than any double-edged sword..." (Hebrews 4:12)! So make it a goal to incorporate scriptures into your prayers. You don't know which scriptures to use? Try this. Highlight your favorite prayer verses in your Bible with a marker. Then pray down through your Bible!

And here's another idea. Try inserting people's names into different verses. Do a trial run through Colossians 1:9-10. You'll love praying for your friends and family in this exciting—and easy—way!

5. *Borrow from the prayers of others*—Of course you'll want to pray your own prayers. But your praying shouldn't stop there. Expand! Grow! Read and pray through the written prayers of others. The powerful prayers of others can be used to bombard heaven like heavy artillery. They help us grow in our prayer skills and passion, and improve our "prayer language" by their eloquence. (To help you, I've included several titles of books of prayers in the back of this book.)

6. *Open and close each day with a time of prayer*—A favorite psalm of mine calls us to declare God's "lovingkindness *in the morning*" and His "faithfulness *every night*" (Psalm 92:2). Morning and evening prayers have been labeled "dawn and dusk bookends."

"Prayer is the key of the morning and the bolt of the night."[1]

Morning and evening. You can develop the habit of beginning and ending each day with prayer. First thing...and last thing! First word...and last word! They belong to God.

7. *Get inspired by the biographies of others who prayed*—Have you guessed yet that I have a passion for reading the biographies of people who prayed? I have a bookshelf full of books about the prayer-journeys God's people have

taken with Him down through the centuries. Each person I journey alongside becomes a friend, a teacher, a model, and a spiritual coach.

I encourage you to do the same thing. But try to take your reading a step further. *Journal* what you're learning! Copy out the most moving passages and quotes from these books. Yes, I mark in my books, but I can't always carry the books with me. However, I can carry my journal any-where...and then sit back and read it over and over again.

(And here's another P.S.: I've included several of these book titles in the back of this book. Start with *Stepping Heavenward* because it's a diary that a young woman began on her fourteenth birthday and wrote in for 20-plus years.)

8. *Study the prayers of the Bible*—I've been sharing a lot of my "favorites" in this book—favorite quotes, stories, scrip-tures, books and authors, heroes of the faith, and prayer practices. But nothing is more powerful in the Prayer Depart-ment than the actual prayers recorded in the Bible.

For instance, the prayer of Mary, the mother of our Lord Jesus (Luke 1:46-55) is referred to as "Mary's Magnificat." Like the "Lord's Prayer" prayed by Jesus, you can learn a lot about prayer by reading this inspired worship prayer. Mary...

 verbalized her personal joy in the Lord's work in her life (verses 46-48),

 exalted the person of God and His work "from generation to generation" (verses 49-50), praised God for His dealings with mankind (verses 51-53), and

 pointed to God's mercy in fulfilling the covenant promise He made to "His servant Israel" (verses 54-55).

9. *Follow through with your resolve: No decision made without prayer*—Your first decision each day must be to pray. This choice will provide you with the time and opportunity to follow through. As you pray over your decisions, God will lead you to find and fulfill His will for your time, your day, and your life.

Amazingly, once time is spent making decisions in prayer, your time is better managed, spent, and saved as a result of walking in God's will. So never forget: *No decision made without prayer!*

10. *Feed your heart and mind with God's Word*—The Bible is the major stimulus for our prayer-life. Through it God speaks to us and fills our hearts and minds with spiritual truths. Prayer is a spiritual work, and no other book can inspire the spiritual work of prayer like the spiritual power of the Bible.

Think about it. Practically speaking, *nothing going in, equals nothing going out.* When we don't read God's Word and expose ourselves to its purity and power, we usually don't think about God and, therefore, we usually don't pray.

Also, *trivia going in, equals trivia going out.* When you hear a person talk trivia (about the latest TV talk show, movie news, gossip), you know what they are feeding on.

And the same goes for "trash"! *Trash going in, equals trash going out!*

But *God's Word going in, equals God's Word going out.* In the case of Mary and her "Magnificat," something was—and had been—going in...for years! And that something was God's law and the knowledge of His dealings with His people. Mary's heart and soul (and remember she, too, was a teenager!) were saturated with God's Word. How do we know this? Because it leaked out of her lips! Because her worship prayer contains about 15 references to Old Testament scriptures. Mary's heart and soul were filled-to-overflowing with God's holy Word. And overflow it did! Her praise and prayer came gushing forth as she "glorified" the God she loved and knew so well through His Word.

My Checklist for Prayer

✓ *Learn*...to leave things undone—Our Number One priority is God, and that includes time spent with Him. All things related to nurturing our relationship with Him—like prayer!—should be first on our "to-do" list. I had to learn that as soon as my husband was off to work and my girls were off to school, the first thing I had to do was pray. It was the only way I could ensure that the most important things—time in God's Word and prayer—got done first! *Then* came everything else in my day.

And it was a struggle! Devotional writer Oswald Chambers understood this well. He writes, We can hinder the time that should be spent with God by remembering we have other things to do. I haven't time. Of course you have not time! Take time! Strangle some other interest and make time to realize that the center of power in your life is the Lord Jesus Christ."[2]

Ask yourself the question, What do I do each day that I think is more important than spending time with God in prayer? The answer, of course, is *nothing!* And so we learn to leave lesser things undone...and pray!

> "Prayer does not fit us for the greater work; prayer *is* the greater work"![3]

I've said it before—we are extremely busy women! Make a list of the things that keep you from praying. Then read Luke 10:38-42. How will you begin to choose what is better—to choose "the thing" that "will not be taken away" from you?

✓ *Learn*...to switch disciplines—As I began to pray regularly, I had to learn to switch disciplines. I had to learn to take a discipline that was already a part of my life and add the new discipline of prayer *ahead of* it.

Let me explain. If you already have the discipline of reading or studying your Bible in place, that discipline is already a part of your life. It's a habit. So now, what you need to do is put prayer *ahead of* your other discipline. Put prayer *in front of* the discipline that's already in place. It takes some doing—and some discipline—but you can learn to leave other things undone until you take care of one of the most important things in your life—answering God's call to prayer.

List some of the things you do every day at the same time. Get up? Do homework? Go to a part-time job? Go to a practice? How can you fit prayer ahead of one of these "disciplines"?

✓   *Learn…*to combine disciplines—I recently met a woman, a "baby Christian," who told me when her time of prayer was. Sandy was going through physical therapy for an injury and had to ride an exercycle for 15 minutes a day at her therapist's treatment center. She said she decided to designate that 15 minutes as her prayer time! Here was a new Christian who had already gone to work on developing the habit of prayer...and had learned to combine her disciplines!

I personally combine walking each day with praying and memorizing Scripture...whether I walk outside or on a treadmill. What other discipline could you combine with prayer? And what do you need to do to prepare to use that time for prayer?

✎ Answering God's Call to You

Dear one, you (and I) are called to pray...period. You are to pray alone, to shut your door and pray to your Father in secret (Matthew 6:6). You are to pray with a handful of faithful others, like Daniel probably did with his three friends (Daniel 1:17-20) and like Paul and Silas did (Acts 16:25). And you are to pray along with others as a corporate body like the disciples of Christ did while gathered in an upper room (Acts 1:13-15). As we'll see in our final chapter, prayer is all-encompassing. It is to be such a vital part of your life that you are praying at all times, in all ways, for all people. (Oh, what joy!)

As we are bringing our thoughts to a close on this most important topic—that of developing the habit of prayer—

please, oh please, do these two things to improve your personal prayer-life:

❀ Do what you must to ensure that you pray daily,
   regularly, habitually.

❀ Do remember that prayer is not about you. It is
   about God, and about your relationship with God,
   and about your walk with God, and about your
   being a woman after God's own heart.

So pray, dear heart! Answer God's call to prayer. Do
whatever it takes to make
your desire to pray a reality.
Do whatever you must to
develop the habit of prayer.

"Prayer crowns God with the honor
and glory due to His name."[4]

Would You Like to Know More?
Check It Out!

List the ten ways to improve your prayer-life and look up the corresponding Bible references. Then write out what you have done or plan to do about each one. Also share how you have been blessed or seen God work with each of these steps as you have begun answering God's call to prayer.

1.

2.

3.

4.

5.

6.

7.

8.

9.

10.

My List of Things I Don't Want to Forget...
...from This Chapter

When You Are Anywhere and at Any Time...Pray!

We did it! We made it to the end of our book about a woman's call to prayer and about our desire to answer God's call. As we look back together, I hope the following truths were communicated to your heart.

Biblical—First and foremost, my prayer throughout this book was to emphasize what is biblical. I wanted us to see a little of what the Bible teaches about prayer. I hope you now have a better understanding and more insights into prayer (although, as we learned, prayer "is beyond our limited human understanding" and "is a topic too deep for the human intellect"[1]).

Practical—I also prayed as I shared the practical elements concerning prayer. I am a nuts-and-bolts-type person. I love studying the Bible—it tells me *what* it is I am to do. But I also want to know *how* to put the *what* into practice...immediately. I have a desire to know how to do what it is I am learning in the Bible.

That's why I included the "My Checklist for Prayer" after each body of teaching. And that's also why I included the reproducible "My Prayer Calendar" at the back of this book. (Have you been using it all along the way? If so, I'm sure you can see progress as you've moved forward on your journey into prayer!)

Beneficial—Then I prayed that what I wrote would be beneficial. My constant prayer has been that your prayer-life will be enhanced, strengthened, sweetened, and bettered. For oh, what glory and honor such a life of prayer will bring to our God!

Mechanical—All the way through this book I trust the undercurrent of my prayers was evident as I sought to communicate that prayer is *not* to be mechanical. My greatest fear is that in my effort to share what the Bible teaches about prayer you may have been discouraged from realizing the simplicity of prayer. In no way do I want you to think that following a formula + jumping through a series of spiritual hoops = prayer!

Natural—Prayer is to be natural. True, prayer is hard work, a spiritual discipline. It must, like anything of value, be tended, cultivated, and cared for. But prayer should be natural. It should flow from your heart to God's. God has built into our hearts and souls a desire to pray, to communicate with Him, to talk to and seek fellowship with Him as our Father. Indeed, we have much to talk over with our God!

When we are afraid, we talk it over with our Protector.

 When we are hurting, we talk it over with our Comforter.

 When we have been mistreated or wrongfully accused, we talk it over with our Advocate.

 When we have a need, we talk it over with our Provider.

Simple—As we close this volume about developing a more meaningful prayer-life, I want to leave you with this simple thought: You can—and are to—pray anywhere, at any time, and at all times! How's that for simplicity? God has made it possible for you to be successful in your desire to pray. You can...

...pray always (Ephesians 6:18), and

...pray without ceasing (1 Thessalonians 5:17).

You Can Pray Anywhere!

Do you realize that you and I can pray anywhere? Neither posture nor place is to limit our praying. It's amazing that we can be in a class at school, at a ball game, listening to a friend talk to us in person or on the phone, exercising, driving a car...well,

> "The man who does all his praying on his knees does not pray enough."[2]

you name it, and whatever it is we are doing, we can pray at the same time.

The very act of praying makes us more wise, sympathetic, discerning, godly, and spiritually alert. We don't miss a thing! In fact, everything we are doing is bettered by the act of prayer.

Even in sadness or when we are hurting or confused by something that is going on in our lives, we can continue to function in a noble way and a gracious manner because we are praying.

> "Certain thoughts are prayers. There are moments when, whatever be the attitude of the body, the soul is on its knees."[3]

You Can Pray at Any Time!

How busy are you? I think I can guess. You're so busy you don't have time to think about how to answer this question, right? But you and I can thank God that because He is everywhere and because of the indwelling of the Holy Spirit in our lives, we can reach out and touch God at any time through our prayers.

> "Forgive us for thinking that prayer is a waste of time, and help us to see that without prayer our work is a waste of time."[4]

Here's a look at another woman who was very busy. Although her lifestyle probably differs from yours, her attitude—and practices—should apply to your life today.

How one woman prayed without ceasing—It seems that a number of ministers were assembled for the discussion of difficult questions; and, among others, it was asked how the command to "pray without ceasing" could be complied with. Various suppositions were stated; and at length, one of the number was appointed to write an essay upon it, to be read at the next meeting. This assignment being over-heard by a servant, she exclaimed, "What! A whole month waiting to tell the meaning of that text? It is one of the eas-iest and best texts in the Bible."

"Well, well!" said an old minister. "Mary, what can you say about it? Let us know how you understand it. Can you pray all the time?"

"Oh, yes, sir!"

"What! When you have so many things to do?"

"Why, sir, the more I have to do, the more I can pray."

"Indeed! Well, Mary, do let us know how it is; for most people think otherwise."

"Well, sir," said the girl,

"when I first open my eyes in the morning, I pray, 'Lord, open the eyes of my understanding;'

and while I am dressing, I pray that I may be clothed with the robe of righteousness; and,

when I have washed me, I ask for the washing of regeneration; and,

as I begin to work, I pray that I may have strength equal to my day;

when I begin to kindle up the fire, I pray that God's work may revive in my soul; and, as I sweep out the house, I pray that my heart may be cleansed from all its impurities; and,

while preparing and partaking of breakfast, I desire to be fed with the hidden manna and the sincere milk of the Word; and,

as I am busy with the little children, I look up to God as my Father, and pray for the spirit of adoption, that I may be his child: and so on all day.

Every thing I do furnishes me with a thought for prayer."

Needless to say, after Mary's little "exposition" on the theology of prayer, the essay was not considered necessary![5]

It's true that you and I can answer God's call to pray from anywhere and at any time. And it's true, as sweet Mary put it, that the more a busy woman has to do, the more she can pray! That is…if our hearts are turned upward! That is…if we are thinking about God!

From my own experience, I've noticed that the heart that prays *is* the heart that is turned upward. The heart that prays *is* the heart that is thinking about God, that is relating everything that happens every minute throughout the day to God. It is when I am in the habit of praying each day that, lo and behold, miracle of miracles, that habit leads to praying all the time…everywhere…for all things…for everything!

You Can Pray All the Time!

You can pray anywhere, and you can pray any time. But you also need to be praying *all* the time! Do you remember God's two commands shared earlier in this chapter?

Pray always (Ephesians 6:18).

Pray without ceasing (1 Thessalonians 5:17).

In other words, you are to be praying all the time...to make your every breath a prayer. As one of my pastors loved to say, prayer is "spiritual breathing." You take a breath in...and a prayer goes out!

I would have to say that during the months I've been immersed in researching and writing this book about prayer and the practice of prayer, the main impact on my life has been being conscious of praying always. Actually, prayer has become an unconscious act. It seems like, wherever I go, I am lifting up the people around me or the event I'm involved in to the Lord through prayer.

For instance, one morning while I was driving somewhere, there was a terrible accident on one of the freeways. The newscasters were talking so coldly as they reported that it was a fatal accident. It was kind of like, "Well, as soon as someone gets the bodies out of there, and the wreckage cleared away, traffic can flow smoothly again."

And you know, I just started praying about the soul of the person who had died. *Was that person a believer?* I also thought, *That person has family members somewhere!* and I began praying for the relatives. I started praying that God would receive glory and honor through a fatal traffic accident and a jammed freeway filled with frustrated people!

Dear praying heart, everywhere you go, if you think of a person, pray. If you see a person (a new student at school or church, a clerk, a neighbor, a homeless man or woman, a young mom pushing a stroller, a soldier being interviewed on the news), pray. If you know about something that's going on in a person's life, pray. If you have an "enemy," pray. Always be "praying always"...like these people did!

> "Are you focusing on a person's faults, or are you lifting that person before the Father?"

Mary Slessor—I once read a diary entry in Mary Slessor's journal. She was a single, nineteenth-century Scottish missionary to Africa who wrote, "My life is one long daily, hourly record of answered prayer. For physical health, for mental overstrain, for guidance given marvelously, for errors and dangers averted, for enmity to the gospel subdued, for food provided at the exact hour needed, for everything that goes to make up life and my poor service to my Savior."[6]

One long daily, hourly prayer! Yes!

John Fletcher—It was the custom of John Fletcher of Madeley, England, never to meet a Christian without saying, "Friend, do I meet you praying?" This unusual salutation reminded the person that his life should be an unbroken expression of prayer and fellowship with God.[7]

An unbroken expression of prayer and fellowship with God! Yes!

Stonewall Jackson—Confederate General "Stonewall" Jackson is described as a man of prayer. He said, "I have so fixed the habit of prayer in my mind that I never raise a glass of water to my lips without asking God's blessing, never seal a letter without putting a word of prayer under that seal, never take a letter to the post without a brief sending of my thoughts heavenward."[8]

"I have so fixed the habit of prayer in my mind...." Yes!

The message is clear, isn't it? We are to take *every* opportunity, during *whatever* is happening, and through *every* event of daily life, to pray...*all* the time. And we can do it, no matter what is transpiring. May the following prayer become yours as you call upon the Lord continually!

Lord...
>   Awaken in us the realization
>   That we need to call on You continually....
>   Teach us to have hearts that pray.
>   Teach us to keep ourselves focused on You.
>   To set up an altar in our hearts,
>   Where our soul might call out to
>   You continually. Amen.[9]

My Checklist for Prayer

✓   *Pray*—The Bible tells you to pray faithfully, fervently, always, without ceasing, continually. Pray, too, when you are in trouble, when you are disappointed by others, when you are hurting, when you are worshiping, when you are worried, when you are overwhelmed, when you are in need, and when you must make a decision. Whatever is happening, you name it...you are to pray! Prayer and praying is the foremost action of a woman—old or young!—who is serious about God's call on her life.

The hardest part about "praying always" is to remember to pray always. What can you do to remember to "think pray" all day long? (Will it be a sticky note? A special bracelet or ring? A scripture you repeat throughout the day? Go ahead and think about it. What will it be?)

✓ *Praise*—I have not focused specifically on praise in this book because the subject of praise could be a book in itself. (Hmmm, I wonder...?) But praise is yet another way we worship God. So during your times of prayer, lift your praise to Him who is most worthy of it! Give praise to "the glory of His grace" (Ephesians 1:6). "Praise our God, all you His servants and those who fear Him, both small and great!" (Revelation 19:5). Let your praise flow outward and upward. It will change your outlook on life!

Read Mary's words of praise in Luke 1:46-55. And read Hannah's words of praise in 1 Samuel 2:1-10.

What praise phrases do you like best from these women's prayers of praise to God? List them, take them, use them, and make them your own!

✓ *Proceed*—How can you become a woman who answers God's call to prayer? How can you make your desire to pray a reality? How can you do a better job of talking to God about your life? In a word, *proceed*...full speed ahead! Proceed to do what you've learned about prayer in this book. Proceed in following God's formula for prayer. Proceed toward finding God's will through prayer. Proceed in developing the habit of prayer. And above all, proceed in your efforts to pray from your heart!

Now, what will your first step be from this day forward?

Would You Like to Know More? Check It Out!

Read Nehemiah 2:1-10.

What was Nehemiah doing (verse 1)?

What question did the king ask (verses 2-4)?

What did Nehemiah do right away (verse 4)?

What were the results (verses 5-10)?

Read again the example of the servant named Mary and her practice of prayer. Which of her prayer habits do you already practice? Which of her prayer habits could you start doing?

Read Ephesians 6:18. What commands are given regarding prayer?

❀

❀

How can you begin to order your life more around God and His desires so that you can make prayer your first response to every situation throughout your days?

My List of Things I Don't Want to Forget...
...from This Chapter

Answering
God's Call to
Prayer

A Dazzling Prayer-Life

Throughout this book I've referred to prayer as a jewel. All along the way, you and I have been examining and admiring the many splendid facets of the precious gem of our prayers. They combine to make the jewel something special indeed—something that blazes forth and lights up your life and the lives of those you pray for, live with, and encounter! And now I want to focus one final time on prayer as a gemstone and on answering God's call to prayer.

As you know, diamonds are said to be a girl's best friend. So let's use a diamond as our jewel of choice. In my lifetime, I've seen two of the world's largest, most famous diamonds, each time while traveling with my husband on one of his ministry trips. One was the Star of Africa, the largest cut diamond in existence. It is set in the British royal scepter, which Jim and I viewed in the Tower of London. This pear-shaped stone "weighs in" at 530.2 carats! The other was the Hope Diamond, the largest deep-blue diamond in the world, which we saw in the National Museum of Natural History at the Smithsonian Institute in Washington, D.C. (We almost didn't stay to see this one because the line was so long. But the wait was well worth it!)

But, my dear journeying friend, please realize that scientists believe brilliant, priceless diamonds like these were formed underground at depths greater than 93 miles and some as deep as 420 miles beneath the earth's surface. And so it is with an even greater jewel—your prayer-life. The holy habit of prayer is formed underground, hidden from sight, "alone with the Eternal."

Why does the formation of a diamond require such incredible recesses? Because crystallization requires pressures and temperatures that only occur at such tremendous depths. And, oh, is that ever true of your glistening prayer-life! The more pressure, the better. The more heat, the better. Such uncomfortable conditions can only make your life of prayer more dazzling. For it is the pressures of life that press us upon God, that move us to lean upon Him...and to seek His power and might in our weaknesses.

So purpose to answer God's call to you to pray. Purpose to hide away with Him in prayer...daily. Doing so will change you. It will change your relationships. And it will change your life. Diamonds are the hardest substance on the earth. And you, dear one, will resemble a diamond when you gather up the conditions and concerns of your life and "take them to the Lord in prayer." You will become, in a good sense, tough, solid, powerful, confident, full-of-faith.

So, dear one, don't cave in under pressure! Don't give in to life's troubles. Don't disintegrate into a puddle of tears and depression. Instead take Jesus' advice to heart. He said you "always ought to pray and not lose heart" (Luke 18:1). Answer His call to prayer! Make it your lifestyle!

A Prayer for Living Out God's Plan

1. *Pray over your priorities*—"Lord, what is Your will for me at this time in my life?"

2. *Plan through your priorities*—"Lord, what must I do today to accomplish Your will?"

3. *Prepare a schedule based on your priorities*—"Lord, when should I do the things that live out these priorities today?"

4. *Proceed to implement your priorities*—"Lord, thank You for giving me Your direction for my day."

5. *Purpose to check your progress*—"Lord, I only have a limited time left in my day. What important tasks do I need to focus on for the remainder of the day?"

6. *Prepare for tomorrow*—"Lord, how can I better live out Your plan for my life tomorrow?"

7. *Praise God at the end of the day*—"Lord, thank You for a meaningful day, for 'a day well spent,' for I have offered my life and this day to You as a 'living sacrifice.'"[1]

Suggested Books of Prayers

The Harper Collins Book of Prayers —A Treasury of Prayers Through the Ages, comp. Robert Van deWeyer. Edison, NJ: Castle Books, 1997.

The One Year® Book of Personal Prayer. Wheaton, IL: Tyndale House Publishers, Inc., 1991.

The Prayers of Susanna Wesley, edited and arranged by W.L. Doughty, Clarion Classics. Grand Rapids, MI: Zondervan Publishing House, 1984.

Elizabeth Prentiss. *Stepping Heavenward.* Amityville, NY: Calvary Press, 1993. The diary of a woman's life and prayers begun at age 14.

The Valley of Vision—A Collection of Puritan Prayers and Devotions, edited by Arthur Bennett. Carlisle, PA: The Banner of Truth Trust, 1999.

Notes

An Invitation to Become a Young Woman of Prayer

1. J.D. Douglas, *The New Bible Dictionary* (Grand Rapids, MI: Wm. B. Eerdmans Publishing Co., 1978), p. 1019.

Chapter 1—Beginning the Journey into Prayer

1. *God's Words of Life for Teens* (Grand Rapids, MI: Zondervan Corporation, 2000), p. 141.
2. A.A. Milne, "Vespers," from *When We Were Very Young* (New York: E.P. Dutton and Co. and Methuen Children's Books Ltd., date unknown).
3. William Law, source unknown.

Chapter 2—What Keeps Me from Praying

1. From the hymn "Turn Your Eyes upon Jesus" by Helen H. Lemmel.
2. Adapted from Paul S. Rees, as quoted in Albert M. Wells Jr., comp., *Inspiring Quotations: Comtemporary and Classified* (Nashville: Thomas Nelson Publishers, 1988), p. 160.
3. Eleanor Doan, *Speaker's Sourcebook* (Grand Rapids, MI: Zondervan Publishing Company, 1988), p. 197.

Chapter 3—When You Are in Trouble or in Need...Pray!

1. Terry W. Glaspey, *Pathway to the Heart of God* (Eugene, OR: Harvest House Publishers, 1998), p. 13.
2. *World Shapers—A Treasury of Quotes from Great Missionaries,* quoting Peter Deyneka, Founder of Slavic Gospel Association (Wheaton, IL: Harold Shaw Publishers, 1991), p. 49.

Chapter 4—When You Are Disappointed or Hurting...Pray!

1. Curtis Vaughn, *The New Testament from 26 Translations* (Grand Rapids, MI: Zondervan Publishing House, 1967), p. 771.
2. Herbert Lockyer, *All the Prayers of the Bible* (Grand Rapids, MI: Zondervan Publishing House, 1973), p. 64.
3. D.L. Moody, *Notes from My Bible and Thoughts from My Library,* quoting Cuyler (Grand Rapids, MI: Baker Book House, 1979), p. 93.
4. Romans 3:23; 1 Corinthians 10:12; 1 John 1:8.

5. Joseph Scriven, "What a Friend We Have in Jesus," 1855.

Chapter 5—When You Are Worried...Pray!

1. Fritz Rienecker, *A Linguistic Key to the Greek New Testament—Volume 2* (Grand Rapids, MI: Zondervan Publishing House, 1981), p. 21.
2. M.R. DeHaan and Henry G. Bosch, *Bread for Each Day* (Grand Rapids, MI: Zondervan Publishing House, 1980), December 11.
3. *Life Application Bible Commentary—Romans* (Wheaton, IL: Tyndale House Publishers, Inc., 1992), p. 164.

Chapter 6—When You Must Make a Decision...
Pray for Faith and Wisdom!

1. Author unknown, quoted in Eleanor Doan, *Speaker's Sourcebook* (Grand Rapids, MI: Zondervan Publishing House, 1988), p. 283.
2. *Checklist for Life for Teens* (Nashville: Thomas Nelson Publishers Publishers, 2002), p. 226.
3. Doan, *Speaker's Sourcebook,* quoting Edward Payton, p. 192.

Chapter 7—When You Must Make a Decision...
Pray for Understanding!

1. Roy B. Zuck, *The Speaker's Quote Book,* quoting Charles Neilsen (Grand Rapids, MI: Kregel Publications, 1997), p. 409.
2. Ibid., p. 110.
3. Ibid., pp. 110-11.

Chapter 8—The Time—and Times—of Prayer

1. Sherwood Eliot Wirt and Kersten Beckstrom, *Topical Encyclopedia of Living Quotations,* quoting Paul S. Rees (Minneapolis: Bethany House Publishers, 1982), p. 181.
2. William Law, as quoted in Terry W. Glaspey, *Pathway to the Heart of God* (Eugene, OR: Harvest House Publishers, 1998), p. 152.
3. "The Difference Prayer Makes," author unknown, in Eleanor Doan, *Speaker's Sourcebook* (Grand Rapids, MI: Zondervan Publishing House, 1988), p. 198. Note: Internet source credits Grace L. Naessens for this poem.

Chapter 9—The Place and Posture of Prayer

1. Ruth Bell Graham, "Especially for You," *Decision,* vol. 43, no. 9, September 2002, p. 42.
2. S.D. Gordon, *Quiet Talks on Prayer* (Grand Rapids, MI: Fleming H. Revell, 1980), pp. 150-58.

3. Herbert Lockyer, *All the Prayers of the Bible* (Grand Rapids, MI: Zondervan Publishing House, 1973), p. 265.

4. Sandra Goodwin, "Traveling on My Knees," as cited in Paul Lee Tan, *Encyclopedia of 7700 Illustrations* (Winona Lake, IN: BMH Books, 1979), p. 1038.

5. Sam Walter Foss (1858–1911), "The Prayer of Cyrus Brown."

Chapter 10—How Can I Learn to Pray?

1. Eleanor L. Doan, *Speaker's Sourcebook* (Grand Rapids, MI: Zondervan Publishing House, 1988), p. 191.

2. Harry Verploegh, ed., *Oswald Chambers—The Best from All His Books* (Nashville: Oliver Nelson/Thomas Nelson Publishers, 1987), p. 359.

3. Doan, *Speaker's Sourcebook,* quoting Oswald Chambers, author's emphasis, p. 192.

4. Frank S. Mead, *12,000 Religious Quotations,* quoting Thomas Benton Brooks (Grand Rapids, MI: Baker Book House, 2000), p. 337.

Chapter 11—When You Are Anywhere and at Any Time...Pray!

1. Terry W. Glaspey, quoted in Terry Glaspey, *Pathway to the Heart of God* (Eugene, OR: Harvest House Publishers, 1998), p. 133.

2. Eleanor L. Doan, *Speaker's Sourcebook* (Grand Rapids, MI: Zondervan Publishing House, 1988), p. 193.

3. Frank S. Mead, *12,000 Religious Quotations,* quoting Victor Hugo (Grand Rapids, MI: Baker Book House, 2000), p. 341.

4. Peter Marshall, as quoted in Roy B. Zuck, *The Speaker's Quote Book* (Grand Rapids, MI: Kregel Publications, 1997), p. 298.

5. Elon Foster, *6000 Sermon Illustrations* (Grand Rapids, MI: Baker Book House, 1992), p. 511.

6. Vinita Hampton and Carol Plueddemann, *World Shapers: A Treasury of Quotes from Great Missionaries* (Wheaton, IL: Harold Shaw Publishers, 1991), p. 46.

7. Roy B. Zuck, *The Speaker's Quote Book,* quoting "Our Daily Bread", p. 294, (February 21, 2004).

8. Ian Bounds, source unknown.

9. Glaspey, *Pathway to the Heart of God*, p. 133.

A Dazzling Prayer-Life

1. Elizabeth George, *Life Management for Busy Women* (Eugene, OR: Harvest House Publishers, 2002), p. 239.

My Prayer Calendar*

Jan.	Feb.	Mar.	Apr.	May	June
1	1	1	1	1	1
2	2	2	2	2	2
3	3	3	3	3	3
4	4	4	4	4	4
5	5	5	5	5	5
6	6	6	6	6	6
7	7	7	7	7	7
8	8	8	8	8	8
9	9	9	9	9	9
10	10	10	10	10	10
11	11	11	11	11	11
12	12	12	12	12	12
13	13	13	13	13	13
14	14	14	14	14	14
15	15	15	15	15	15
16	16	16	16	16	16
17	17	17	17	17	17
18	18	18	18	18	18
19	19	19	19	19	19
20	20	20	20	20	20
21	21	21	21	21	21
22	22	22	22	22	22
23	23	23	23	23	23
24	24	24	24	24	24
25	25	25	25	25	25
26	26	26	26	26	26
27	27	27	27	27	27
28	28	28	28	28	28
29	29	29	29	29	29
30		30	30	30	30
31		31		31	

* See p. 19 in chapter 1 under "Checklist for Prayer" (third checkmark section) for instructions in using this encouraging calendar.

Date I Began _____

July	Aug.	Sept.	Oct.	Nov.	Dec.
1	1	1	1	1	1
2	2	2	2	2	2
3	3	3	3	3	3
4	4	4	4	4	4
5	5	5	5	5	5
6	6	6	6	6	6
7	7	7	7	7	7
8	8	8	8	8	8
9	9	9	9	9	9
10	10	10	10	10	10
11	11	11	11	11	11
12	12	12	12	12	12
13	13	13	13	13	13
14	14	14	14	14	14
15	15	15	15	15	15
16	16	16	16	16	16
17	17	17	17	17	17
18	18	18	18	18	18
19	19	19	19	19	19
20	20	20	20	20	20
21	21	21	21	21	21
22	22	22	22	22	22
23	23	23	23	23	23
24	24	24	24	24	24
25	25	25	25	25	25
26	26	26	26	26	26
27	27	27	27	27	27
28	28	28	28	28	28
29	29	29	29	29	29
30	30	30	30	30	30
31	31		31		31

Personal Notes

Personal Notes

Personal Notes

Books by Elizabeth George

- Beautiful in God's Eyes
- Breaking the Worry Habit…Forever
- Finding God's Path Through Your Trials
- Following God with All Your Heart
- Life Management for Busy Women
- Loving God with All Your Mind
- A Mom After God's Own Heart
- Quiet Confidence for a Woman's Heart
- Raising a Daughter After God's Own Heart
- The Remarkable Women of the Bible
- Small Changes for a Better Life
- Walking with the Women of the Bible
- A Wife After God's Own Heart
- A Woman After God's Own Heart*
- A Woman After God's Own Heart* Deluxe Edition
- A Woman After God's Own Heart*— A Daily Devotional
- A Woman After God's Own Heart* Collection
- A Woman After God's Own Heart DVD and Workbook
- A Woman's Call to Prayer
- A Woman's Daily Walk with God
- A Woman's High Calling
- A Woman's Walk with God
- A Woman Who Reflects the Heart of Jesus
- A Young Woman After God's Own Heart
- A Young Woman After God's Own Heart— A Devotional
- A Young Woman's Call to Prayer
- A Young Woman's Guide to Making Right Choices
- A Young Woman's Walk with God

Study Guides

- Beautiful in God's Eyes Growth & Study Guide
- Finding God's Path Through Your Trials Growth & Study Guide
- Following God with All Your Heart Growth & Study Guide
- Life Management for Busy Women Growth & Study Guide
- Loving God with All Your Mind Growth & Study Guide
- A Mom After God's Own Heart Growth & Study Guide
- The Remarkable Women of the Bible Growth & Study Guide
- Small Changes for a Better Life Growth & Study Guide
- A Wife After God's Own Heart Growth & Study Guide
- A Woman After God's Own Heart* Growth & Study Guide
- A Woman's Call to Prayer Growth & Study Guide
- A Woman's High Calling Growth & Study Guide
- A Woman's Walk with God Growth & Study Guide
- A Woman Who Reflects the Heart of Jesus Growth & Study Guide

Children's Books

- A Girl After God's Own Heart
- God's Wisdom for Little Girls
- A Little Girl After God's Own Heart

Books by Jim George

- 10 Minutes to Knowing the Men and Women of the Bible
- The Bare Bones Bible* Facts
- The Bare Bones Bible* Handbook
- The Bare Bones Bible* Handbook for Teens
- A Husband After God's Own Heart
- A Leader After God's Own Heart
- A Man After God's Own Heart
- The Man Who Makes a Difference
- The Remarkable Prayers of the Bible
- A Young Man After God's Own Heart

Books by Jim & Elizabeth George

- God Loves His Precious Children
- God's Wisdom for Little Boys
- A Little Boy After God's Own Heart

A Young Woman After God's Own Heart

What does it mean to pursue God's heart in your everyday life? It means understanding and following God's perfect plan for your friendships, your faith, your family relationships, and your future. Learn how to...

- grow close to God
- enjoy meaningful relationships
- make wise choices
- become spiritually strong
- build a better future
- fulfill the desires of your heart

As you read along, you'll find yourself caught up in the exciting adventure of a lifetime—that of becoming a woman after God's own heart!

A Young Woman After God's Own Heart
is available at your local Christian bookstore
or can be ordered at:

www.ElizabethGeorge.com

BIBLE STUDIES *for* BUSY WOMEN

A WOMAN AFTER GOD'S OWN HEART® BIBLE STUDIES

Character Studies

Old Testament Studies

New Testament Studies

*E*lizabeth takes women step-by-step through the Scriptures, sharing wisdom she's gleaned from more than 30 years as a women's Bible teacher.

Embracing God's Grace

NEW

About the Author

Elizabeth George is a bestselling author whose passion is to teach the Bible in a way that changes women's lives. She has more than 7 million books in print, including *A Woman After God's Own Heart* and *A Woman's Daily Walk with God*.

For information about Elizabeth, her books, and her ministry, and to sign up to receive her daily devotions, and to join her on Facebook and Twitter, visit her website at:

www.ElizabethGeorge.com